Woodrow Wilson
and the
Politics of
Morality

The Library of American Biography

EDITED BY OSCAR HANDLIN

John Morton Blum

Woodrow Wilson
and the
Politics of Morality

Edited by Oscar Handlin

Little, Brown and Company · *Boston* · *Toronto*

The author wishes to thank the copyright owners for permission to quote from
WOODROW WILSON: LIFE AND LETTERS, by Ray Stannard Baker. Copyright 1927,
1939 by Doubleday & Company, Inc. Reprinted by permission of Mrs. Rachel
Baker Napier and Doubleday & Company, Inc.

Published simultaneously in Canada
by Little, Brown & Company (Canada) Limited

PRINTED IN THE UNITED STATES OF AMERICA

Editor's Preface

Many sensitive Americans who came to maturity in the decades just after the Civil War were troubled by the condition of politics in their time. The great conflict that fell across their youth certainly called attention to the unresolved problems of government, and the number and complexity of those problems grew as the century drew to a close.

The state was an instrument of power; the policeman was the symbol of its ability to command obedience by force. So much was obvious.

But to Americans the state was more than power. It was also a device created by the people scarcely a century before for advancing their common welfare. And how could the people bring into being an instrument of naked power that might be used solely to oppress them? The answer could be only that in a republic the state had power but could use it only toward ends deemed desirable by the common standards of morality.

This was an old question and an old answer. Yet now, as the United States advanced in power, as the functions of government grew more complex and extended beyond

v

the borders of the continent, it was no longer satisfying thus to dispose of the matter. It was more difficult to apply traditional conceptions of morality to the new circumstances than it had been in an innocent past. The men of the 1880's and the 1890's were frightened by the corruption and the ineffectiveness of government and were troubled by the contradictions between the premises and the promises of American life and its reality. After 1898, furthermore, the abrupt involvement in world-wide imperialism made awkward demands upon the framework of old ideas.

This was the great underlying problem of American politics as the nineteenth century gave way to the twentieth. More than any of his contemporaries, Woodrow Wilson would grapple with it. John M. Blum's perceptive analysis reveals the steps of training and career that brought this man to one of the great crises of our time.

OSCAR HANDLIN

Contents

Woodrow Wilson
and the
Politics of
Morality

For My Father

I

"A Longing to Do Immortal Work"

1856–1902

ON THE THIRD FLOOR of his home on S Street
in Washington, in a large four-poster — a replica of the
Lincoln bed in the White House — on Friday, February 1,
1924, Woodrow Wilson lay dying. Outside on the street
motorists and pedestrians stopped for a while to watch
silently the closed house, some with maudlin interest to
identify the callers there, some reverently to await the
word of death. The Chief Justice of the Supreme Court,
the Secretary of War, Wilson's former secretary, several
others left their cards; without a word one woman left six
carnations loosely wrapped in damp green tissue paper. At
the Keith Theatre Saturday night the manager, focusing
on Wilson's vacant seat, urged the audience to pray for the
"great and noble man." As that night wore on a cold wind
drove down the hill at S Street, but many silent watchers
stayed. One veiled woman said a rosary. By nine A.M. on
February 3 some five hundred people, quiet as before, had
gathered. A small boy — the child of a wounded veteran
— placed at the door one pale pink rose. At ten a fur-clad
woman distributed cards inscribed "Peace on earth, good

will to men." Following her lead, fifty of those assembled knelt in silent prayer. At 11:15 Wilson died. His personal physician, voice trembling, informed the crowd. Some wept.

Woodrow Wilson, his mourners felt, had given his life to righteousness. But how many wept for Wilson, how many for righteousness? How many for the lasting peace that Wilson hoped his League of Nations would effect?

Alive, he had not often moved men to tears, though at times his causes had. His intimates, loving him, understood that among masses of men he roused hope and earned admiration but did not win affection. In a replica of Lincoln's bed he died, but in life he had not displayed Lincoln's warm sense of humanity. Instead, and sometimes cruelly, Wilson had subordinated men to causes. When he died men sorrowed, but not spontaneously as they had for Lincoln or as they would for Franklin Roosevelt. Not so much for Wilson did the small boy leave a rose as for his father's wound, for the crusade to make the world safe for democracy, for the war to end war.

Wilson had intended this. From youth he had determined to find principles by which men might justly order their affairs; he had wished to articulate in poetic periods his noble ideals, to identify himself with them, and to govern for them. He had for many years a calm confidence in great things to be accomplished, in his own perception through God of what they were, in his own energy and artistry to communicate them persuasively. So far as his convictions were concerned, once they were formed, discussion was adjourned. He had, he said, a one-track mind. No friend, no matter how beloved, could with impunity oppose him. Not reason, not expediency, not compassion moved him after he defined the right.

Such a man is seldom happy. The intensity of ambition, the pride of righteousness, the faith in triumph preclude contentment. Wilson was a troubled man whose compulsiveness helped him to lead a nation to large achievements and larger hopes, whose self-assurance let him now hurt men to help mankind, now torture principle to vindicate himself. Such a man is hard to love. But such a man can, as Wilson did, mark the minds and souls of other men.

Wilson's is the story of a boy who dreamed of winning glory by great speeches that would move people, parliaments and parties; of a boy with intimations of immortality, a boy who arranged to make his dreams come true. A rare boy. A leader who won great triumphs but lost his most important battle. A tragic man whose aspirations free men still revere but one who placed himself in the way of making those aspirations real.

*   *   *

"Better than a fair country," Wilson once wrote, "is a good parentage." He had both. He was born on December 28, 1856, in Staunton, Virginia, the third child, first son, of Joseph Ruggles and Jessie Woodrow Wilson. Christened Thomas Woodrow Wilson, he grew up in the South, living two years in Staunton, twelve in Augusta, Georgia, two in Columbia, South Carolina. His first recollection was of standing at his father's gateway in Augusta and hearing a passer-by say that Lincoln had been elected and there would be war. He remembered also his father's loyalty to the Confederacy, some episodes of wartime privation, more of the disorder of postwar reconstruction. Never a muddled devotee of the Lost Cause, Wilson nevertheless took pride in the South's war effort just as he rejoiced "in the failure of the Confederacy" because, so he averred, he loved the South. "The only place in the world," he often observed, "where nothing has to be explained to me is the South."

Wilson's father, a Presbyterian minister, was the son of a Scotch-Irish immigrant who prospered in Ohio; Wilson's mother, born in Carlisle, England, was the daughter of one Presbyterian minister, the sister of another, who defied his fundamentalist colleagues by teaching evolution. Jessie Woodrow Wilson, a proud gentlewoman, religious, refined and maternal, gave her son and won from him a love the memories of which, he wrote, seemed "to hallow" his "whole life." From her, he judged, there came to him also a kind of chivalric "love of the best womanhood." Unquestionably he needed at all times woman's sympathy, piety and domesticity to provide an environment in which he could relax, admired. His mother and sisters, later — according to the pattern of his customary family life — his wife and daughters, gave Wilson indispensable emotional support.

Wilson's father was also his first teacher and first friend. The minister's insistence that his son express every idea they discussed in precise language trained the boy not only to use English well but also to take special pleasure in using it. Listening to his father's Sunday sermons and daily prayers, Wilson learned the power of spoken language, assimilated the faith it spoke, worshiped not only the Lord but also the man who described Him. "My son," the minister instructed, "the mind is not a prolix gut to be stuffed." Believing this, his son read closely rather than widely, preferred reflection to research. Quoting this, his son in time constructed a system of education one principle of which was to be done with stuffing. The minister, a moral man,

believed that good conduct graced only an ordered society. His son in time, he felt, preached "a gospel of order, and thus of safety." Wilson dedicated his first book to his father, "the patient guide of his youth, the gracious companion of his manhood, his best instructor." As long as his father lived, Wilson sought his advice. "In his majestic presence," his adult son, a Princeton professor, parent of three children, was a pupil, "an obedient boy."

In spite of war and reconstruction, Wilson's youth was comfortable. The Reverend Dr. Wilson was never wealthy, but he was financially secure and socially accepted. Young Wilson shared the prestige accorded his father's pulpit and, while they lived in Columbia, his father's professorship at the seminary there. He went to school with "nice boys," some of them destined to achieve a measure of celebrity as adults in public or business life. His schoolboy studies he pursued without ardor and mastered without distinction. He developed for ships and the sea a boyish enthusiasm like that of later-day boys about airplanes and the air. He played with sufficient gusto to gain and retain some interest in football and baseball.

But Wilson was not an ordinary boy. His deep religious feeling, his romantic view of knowledge, his intense ambition created within him expectations he always felt compelled to realize. Wilson expressed these qualities in letters and essays he wrote at college and law school, later as a young lawyer and young professor. But just as these qualities penetrated his entire adult life, so did they inhere — unexpressed but always guiding — in his precollege years.

Inheritance and indoctrination made Wilson a Presbyterian; temperament made him an especially devout one — a "Presbyterian priest" in the words of one Roman Catholic politician who had reason to know. The Presbyterians were, Wilson learned, a special people chosen by God to know His purpose and do His will, an elect, an aristocracy of souls predestined to achieve salvation in the next world and to manifest signs of that graceful state in this world. If God's chosen people were to be the instruments of His just intent, so also were they "sinful and selfish" men, responsible to Him and ultimately to be judged by His exacting standards. Wilson's God was, however, accessible, both through prayer, which afforded guidance, and in His revealed word. The Bible, Wilson remarked, "reveals every man to himself as a distinct moral agent, responsible not to men, not even to those men whom he has put over him in authority, but responsible through his own conscience to his Lord and Maker." So persuaded, Wilson daily read the Scripture and daily prayed. In this he found both strength and comfort. He also found occasion to interpret as the Lord's will convictions other men attributed to less remote sources, occasion to hallow and moralize issues other men considered secular and casual.

For any devout man the interpretation of the will of God is difficult to discipline. It was especially so for Woodrow Wilson, for he often relied less upon data to make up his mind than upon intuition. As his academic colleagues were to observe, there was in Wilson a great deal of Ralph Waldo Emerson. A confident, individualistic, sentimental romanticism leavened the sternness of Wilson's religion. This characteristic, common enough among Wilson's generation, particularly affected a middle-class Southern boy who aspired to fame, the son of a man who expected well-turned phrases — pulpit poetry — to turn minds. Wilson as a boy moved by a communion hymn wept in church. As an adult, like many of his contemporaries, he wrote of his love of wife, family or friends with an unashamed sentimental fervor that would embarrass or amuse a later generation. Even in his own day he was something of a period piece, resisting alike the harshness of accelerating industrialism and the rigor of the kind of thinking upon which science and critical realism depended.

The adult Wilson described himself as "an idealist, with the heart of a poet." So too was the sensitive boy who, searching for righteous absolutes in life, responded to conditioned emotions, to a sometimes mawkish sense of beauty, to the stirrings of his soul actuated — so he believed — by its communion with the eternal. Wilson considered man's own spirit the first, best source of ideas. Great statesmen, he concluded as he studied history, had the souls of poets. He sought inspiration, as he believed they had done, in a "long view of human nature" derived more from literature than from empirical data. Not history as professional historians wrote it but history as he felt it formed, as he grew up, his remembrances of things past.

The columns of the New York *Nation* and the *Edinburgh Review,* to which his father subscribed, shaped Wilson's view of affairs and also his ambition. In the year in which he joined the church, his sixteenth year, he hung over his desk a portrait of his hero, William E. Gladstone, perennial prime minister of Victorian England, incomparable public exponent of the Manchesterian political and economic doctrines that the *Nation* and the *Review* espoused. Gladstone's life, the young Wilson judged, had "been one continuous advance, not towards power only . . . but towards truth also." Part of this truth was laissez-faire political economy, the belief that self-adjusting eco-

nomic forces provided the best of all possible economic
worlds; that the best government, therefore, was the gov·
ernment that interfered least with those forces; that a protective tariff on this account was a treacherous device to
confuse the automatic workings of a system decreed by
God. A boy reared in the South, where protection had
long been viewed as a scourge, was immediately prepared
to believe this gospel. Part of the truth toward which
Gladstone advanced was a faith that in a laissez-faire economy virtue made its own reward, that ability and industry
insured prosperity — a faith both generated by and assimilated into the Calvinist ethic of Wilson's religion. This
faith had particular attraction for a young man who aspired to do great things. Part of the truth associated with
Gladstone was a mystic conviction in the superiority and
mission of Anglo-Saxons, their right — as Gladstone saw
it — to imperial dominion in Africa and Asia. This also
Wilson could readily believe. It confirmed the special virtue he attributed to his ancestors, the confidence he felt in
the destiny of a reunited America, the theory he absorbed
in the South that Negroes were inferior beings, the distaste
he harbored for those non-British newcomers to the
United States, whom he blamed in large degree for a deg-
radation of American democracy.

Gladstone's advance toward power provided Wilson
with an enduring symbol for his own ambition. The boy
dreamed of being the prime minister of a cabinet of English gentlemen, of being the articulate leader of a party
subscribing to and ennobled by his purposes, the admired
orator, effective alike debating with his peers or instructing his constituency. All Wilson's life this dream lasted,
altered only in detail to fit changing circumstances. It was
"much the most answering thing that he knew."

To make it come true, Wilson began while in his teens to cultivate the art of persuasion, what he was later to call "the deep eloquence which awakens purpose." Through God, through poetic intuition, through a sense of things past as they bore on things present, he would perceive the first principles of political behavior; through a poetry of speech he would persuade men to follow his prescriptions. The adolescent memorized the speeches of great orators and rehearsed them in empty woods and empty chapels, studied words and sounds and cadences, and contrived at every opportunity to organize among his friends mock parliaments where he and they might practice writing laws and constitutions and influencing each other. How susceptible was such a boy, grown up, to confusing belief with truth, substituting words for facts! Consumed with intimations of greatness, identifying fame with nobility, intent on mastering the substance of both and the techniques to guarantee that they be acknowledged, the young Wilson harbored the temptations that let a man become the unseeing victim of his own preferred formulations. So consumed and so compelled, he had also the self-discipline and impatience of ambition, the will and energy that breed success.

More slowly than suited him, more thoroughly than could one less compulsive, more fruitfully than perhaps he realized, he cultivated his youthful garden. Wilson first left home in 1873 to attend Davidson College, a small Presbyterian institution near Charlotte, North Carolina, where he concentrated on the activities of the debating society. Unprepared after a year at Davidson to matriculate at Princeton, he returned home for fifteen months to study. In 1875 he departed again, this time for Princeton. There he barely consented to follow the course of study the college prescribed, focusing instead on those few subjects which promised to prepare him to become an informed and eloquent statesman. Only partly in fun, he informed his classmates when they differed on some issue that he would continue the discussion when he met them in the Senate. He even wrote out a few cards, "Thomas Woodrow Wilson, Senator from Virginia."

Constantly engaged in writing and debating, Wilson set out to learn "the control of other minds by a strange personal influence and power." With one classmate he formed "a solemn covenant . . . that we should acquire knowledge that we might have power; and . . . drill ourselves in all the arts of persuasion, but especially in oratory." Avidly reading British and American history, he confirmed his nascent belief that the history of the United States was but an extension — often unsalubrious — of British history. "Have you ever," he asked a classmate, "thought of the reason for the decline of American oratory?" Wilson had. The decisions of Congress, he concluded, were made in committees where negotiation rather than debate controlled. In Parliament, on the contrary, issues were debated and decided on the floor; there eloquence and, by Wilson's standard, statesmanship persisted. Wilson proposed this thesis in an essay he wrote as a senior; later he developed it in his first book. With some friends at Princeton he also organized a Liberal Debating Club where the "Secretary of State," the head of the "government," presented "bills" for debate and, with his "party," survived or fell depending on whether they "passed." Wilson wrote the constitution for this club; Wilson, inevitably, was the "Secretary of State."

"The profession I chose," Wilson explained four years after he graduated from Princeton, "was politics; the profession I entered was the law. I entered the one because I thought it would lead to the other." With this motive, Wilson matriculated in 1879 at the law school of the University of Virginia. Characteristically, he supplemented his professional studies with drill in "the arts of persuasion." Quickly he made a reputation at the oratorical club. During his vacation he amused himself with the study of pronunciation. He also played with cadence. At his mother's request, he began to sign his name not "Thomas W. Wilson" as he always had, but "T. Woodrow Wilson." This was certainly a more euphonious name for a slightly chivalric Southern senator, a name soon adjusted further when he dropped forever the initial "T." At law school Wilson either did or yearned too much. Poor health, occasioned perhaps more by ambition than by late hours or poor food, forced him to complete his legal studies at home. There, "fairly in love with speech-making," he practiced systematically every day, confessing that "my *end* is a commanding influence in the councils (and counsels) of my country."

First, however, he had to try the law. He began in June, 1882, in partnership with a University of Virginia contemporary at Atlanta, Georgia. Resolved to remain in the South, Wilson chose the city which more than any other represented the new industrialism of the section. "I think," he told a friend, "that to grow up with a new section is no small advantage for one who seeks to gain position and influence." But growing up was hard for Wilson. Attending court "proved very depressing," for he could not, as he put it, "breathe freely . . . in an atmosphere of broken promises, of wrecked estates, of neglected trusts, of unperformed duties." This side of human nature, he concluded, hardened and narrowed him. Without experience in dealing with everyday human problems, the young man wanted none. Intent as he was on commanding the councils of the country and swaying the Senate with his eloquence, Wilson simply had no time or sympathy for the case of a poor Negro caught stealing a hen. Searching for the first principles of persuasion, hoping to discover grand rules for governing groups of men, Wilson had little interest in the petty problems of individuals. He never had a case of his own.

"Success at the bar," Wilson decided, would be "very doubtful and at best long delayed." He was in rather a hurry, and he preferred the triumphs he won during the debates of the Atlanta chapter of the Free Trade Club. He also pursued success as a voluntary witness before the Tariff Commission, which in September, 1882, heard testimony in Atlanta. "Influenced" — as he wrote a friend — "by the consideration" that his speech "would appear in their printed report," Wilson informed the members of the commission that his purpose was "only to say a few words upon the general issue . . . of protection or free trade." He then made a brief and unoriginal case against protection. He did not trouble adequately to sustain theory with fact: one of his statements on the wheat schedule had to be corrected. Yet he was "embarrassed by the smallness and the character of the audience, but more especially by the ill-natured and sneering interruptions of the commissioners." He was meant, he was sure, for higher things. But he was "compensated" for his "discomfort by the . . . compliments of . . . friends and of the press."

"Dependent on intellectual sympathy," Wilson needed such compliments. He relied for them upon those Princeton intimates with whom he corresponded regularly. They shared his admiration of British ways, his disdain for the unwashed, his conviction that proper Princetonians, among others like them, were a genuine elite. But in Georgia, Wilson concluded, "culture" was "very little esteemed." There "the chief end of man" was "to make money," an end he despised, perhaps partly because he needed money badly but could not bring himself to earn it. Recognition, intellectual sympathy, esteem — all these he missed. The law did not appeal.

If there were no parliaments to persuade, there was at least a genteel public devoted — like his friends — to reading the polite periodicals that scolded the parvenus of the Gilded Age. There were also the young men who attended polite colleges. To these Wilson turned. "I want to make myself *an outside force in politics,*" he averred, to "write something that men might delight to read." Abandoning the law in 1883, he applied for admission to the graduate school at the Johns Hopkins University. Although denied a fellowship, he matriculated "to get a special training in historical research and an insight into the most modern literary and political thoughts and methods, in order that my ambition to become an invigorating and enlightening power in the world of political thought and a master . . . of literary art may be the more easy of accomplishment."

Before entering Hopkins Wilson fell in love with Ellen Axson of Rome, Georgia, a young woman who was to command the affectionate admiration of all who knew her. From the time he met her until the day she died, she meant more to Wilson than did any other human being, any dream, any achievement. From her he learned that "a man who lives only for himself has not begun to live." She protected him not only from the world that so often tired him but also, more significantly, from himself. Through the years of their marriage she taught him much about beauty and more about sympathy. Only in her could Wilson confide fully; only she could palliate the deep loneliness that clothed his <u>tense ambition</u>. But even Ellen Axson, particularly in the first years she knew him, could not teach Wilson the things his temperament would not let him learn.

At Hopkins he learned remarkably little. He did assimilate considerable historical data; he did further familiarize himself with Manchesterian economics; he did become aware of new ideas about the significance of the American frontier and of older ones about the organic nature of the state. But he came away from Hopkins without increasing the number or enhancing the insights of his favored generalizations, without improving substantially his capacity to reason — his own test of education. This was not the fault of Hopkins. That university, adapting German graduate techniques to American scholarship, provided the most stimulating environment in the United States for the study of history and political science. The fault was Wilson's. He worked diligently not only on his studies but also, as ever, on oratory. Yet, concentrating on the kind of reading that had always interested him, he learned only what confirmed the beliefs he had brought with him. So history remained for him past politics and politics alone; American history, an extension of the British past; Britain's, an incomparable political system; change, an evolutionary matter to be accepted cautiously. Political leadership remained his goal, oratory and persuasion its devices.

All these ideas Wilson had been nurturing for years; all permeated his first book, *Congressional Government,* written at Hopkins, accepted there as his doctoral dissertation, and published in 1885. For the while he covered the picture of Gladstone with that of Walter Bagehot, British publicist, editor of the *Economist,* expert on the British constitution, influential spokesman of a conservative gospel of order skillfully blended of laissez-faire economics, Darwinian biology, and the current sociology that merged those two. Bagehot, as Wilson kept in mind, had studied law but abandoned it; Bagehot was, within his sphere, a persuasive leader of men. While at Hopkins Wilson mastered both the mind and the style of his new commander in chief.

In Bagehot's manner and in the pattern of Bagehot's *English Constitution,* Wilson wrote his *Congressional Government.* He described how laws were made, how congressional committees worked, who were the congressional decision makers and how they exercised their power. He criticized what seemed to him to be the domination of American government by the legislative branch, which, dividing its business for decision by committees, divided power and avoided responsibility. The British system, he argued, concentrated in the cabinet and in the person of the prime minister both power and responsibility and provided in the debates of the whole Parliament a forum for trenchant discussion of policy. By implication he suggested the United States adopt the British way.

Wilson owed a considerable debt not only to Bagehot but also to American reformers and publicists who for over a decade had been developing the ideas *Congressional Government* elaborated. Like his creditors, Wilson dealt only with political mechanisms, ignoring the social and economic influences on political behavior and congressional activity. Indeed, he did not trouble before writing even once to observe Congress or one of its committees at work. Minimizing the power of the American executive, Wilson failed to take into account the large achievements of such strong Presidents as Jackson and Lincoln. By choice interpreting the Senate as an American House of Lords, Wilson evaluated it as a classless body useful as an undemocratic check to the mass tyranny potentially inherent in the House of Representatives. He had still in mind, clearly, a body of disinterested gentlemen responding to each other's measured oratory. Actually, however, the Senate by 1885 to an alarming degree represented the particular interests of powerful economic groups that arranged the election of many of its members. Desire as much as scholarship molded Wilson's book.

But whatever its shortcomings, *Congressional Government* was for Wilson an almost unmitigated success. The same patrician reformers who had earlier expounded Wilson's theses gave the book enthusiastic reviews. Polite Americans both bought and read a volume that registered their contempt for American politicians and corroborated their belief in British excellences. Didactic but graceful, restrained but haughty, Wilson's mannered prose suitably illuminated his ideas. To a large and influential audience he was, as he had long hoped to be, persuasive. But he was not content. He regretted still forgoing a statesman's career; he regretted that American public service had "no room for such a career . . . for anybody." He concluded, happily, that his "power to write" was designed to further his "power to speak and to organize action." He would "push on: to linger would be fatal."

Push on he did, for seventeen productive years, successively a professor of history at Bryn Mawr until 1888, at Wesleyan until 1890, and a professor of jurisprudence and political economy at Princeton until 1902. In that time he published five books and a multivolume history: *The State* (1889), a textbook on comparative government emphasizing the gradual, orderly, organic growth of political institutions; *Division and Reunion* (1893), a short, impartial account of the Civil War and Reconstruction; *George Washington* (1896), a laudatory and undistinguished biography; *An Old Master and Other Political Essays* (1893) and *Mere Literature* (1896), selections from his essays and addresses; and the *History of the American People* (1902), his five-volume chronicle of essentially political events. Wilson's scholarship was unimpressive, often shallow or derivative. But he did win and hold an increasing audience, for he dignified the preconceptions of upper-middle-class Americans with his professorial sanction in the genteel, often stilted, but flowing prose they liked. So also in his classrooms. Students remembered Wilson as a middling teacher but a superb lecturer. His natural reserve, his inability or disinclination to understand another individual, his private preoccupations made him a poor partner at the other end of an academic log; but his polished elocution served him well behind college or public lecterns. By his own account, he was willing to court favor with groups of people, but he considered it a sacrifice of pride to try to win over one man. "I have a sense of power in dealing with men collectively," he admitted, "which I do not feel always in dealing with them singly."

This sense of power he yearned to test in some post of authority or on some malleable constituency. Neither success in the classroom nor success as an author satisfied his "longing to do immortal work," for such work, he still believed, involved active statesmanship. Twice he applied for appointment as Assistant Secretary of State. Denied this position, for which he had neither adequate experience nor influential support, he intensified his writing and pub-

lic lecturing, addressing himself continually to current issues and brooding over what he considered the bankruptcy
of national leadership.

Wilson, however, had little new to offer. He approved of
the nation's imperialistic ventures, confident that the example of the white man and his imposition of order and
discipline would benefit the Filipinos and Puerto Ricans.
The responsibility for overseas possessions would also, he
suggested, help Americans to learn to rule themselves. He
worried about the growth of large combinations in industry and transportation, recognized the potential dangers in such concentrations of economic power, approved
of the concept of federal regulation so weakly applied by
the Interstate Commerce Act of 1887, but at the same time
opposed proposals for more extensive control of corporations and their activities. Such schemes, he argued, infringed upon the domain of the states, violated the economic liberty of the individual, and threatened therefore
the constitutional system and the economic growth of the
United States.

This ambivalent fear at once of big business and of
regulating it Wilson shared with the majority of the American middle class. He shared also their dismay at the labor
disturbances and agrarian radicalism that attended the
depression of the 1890's. Sensing though he did that
economic conditions provoked this unrest and created the
political attitudes that made William Jennings Bryan the
Democratic presidential candidate in 1896, Wilson nevertheless doubted Bryan's intelligence and sincerity, opposed the unlimited coinage of silver at a ratio to gold of
16–1 (the panacea that Bryan made his own), and voted
not for the Great Commoner but for the candidate of the
rump of conservative Democrats who remained faithful to

gold, states' rights, the open shop and, of course, a tariff
for revenue only.

In place of a program Wilson substituted a beguiling
jargon. What the country needed was a "sincere body of
thought in politics . . . boldly uttered"; he meant that
the country lacked confident but conservative leadership.
He wanted an American Edmund Burke, but one who
could win national elections. Public opinion, he allowed,
had to be truckled to at the end of the nineteenth century, but it also, he insisted, had to be educated, persuaded
by a forceful leader who could perceive the inchoate de-
sires of the community and formulate them in broad, obvious, convincing arguments. Such a leader would possess
poetic insights and poetic talents. "By methods which
would infallibly alienate individuals," he would "master
multitudes." He would reveal to them the wisdom of
tradition, teach them to keep "faith with the past."

If the nation was not ready to accept Wilson's kind of
leadership, Princeton was. The problems of the college
were not those of the country. Princeton needed the guidance of a believer in its past who could be also an imaginative molder of its future. For this role Professor Woodrow
Wilson, hard at work on the methods and purposes of
education, was perhaps unintentionally preparing himself.
Whatever his motive, at the Princeton Sesquicentennial in
1896 Wilson delivered an address, "Princeton in the Nation's Service," which made a compelling campaign document. Princeton, he asserted, had supplied and should supply a trained, disinterested, cultured, vigorous governing
elite. But this was becoming increasingly difficult, for science and scientific method bred among college faculties
and students a contempt for the past. Instruction in literature, history and politics, he believed, especially instruc-

tion in the achievements of English-speaking people, could redress this, could bring back to college education a lost moral force. Because Princeton in particular should be a pre-eminent school of "the progress which conserves," the next Princeton generations should be trained to see a "vision of the true God" and to take "counsel with the elder dead who still live."

Wilson made this message his creed for education. Repeated in various forms during the next five years, it delighted many of his colleagues and most trustees. He was offered a number of college presidencies which he declined. Then, in 1902, Princeton's aging, ineffective president was persuaded to resign, and by a unanimous vote Wilson was elected to succeed him. The first layman to be so honored, he accepted at once, happy to have at last "a sense of position and of definite, tangible tasks." His old visions now focused on the opportunity to lead Princeton to greatness in scholarship and education. As he prepared his inaugural address, Wilson felt, so he wrote his wife, "like a new prime minister getting ready to address his constituents." He had, after all, always felt this way.

Prime Minister of
Princeton
1902-1910

Princeton's best hopes when Wilson became president were its past and his spirit. Education at the college had for some time been unimaginative; administration, lax. Some of the faculty lacked scholarly ability; others, enthusiasm for teaching; many — particularly among the older men — were undistinguished. The curriculum, inhibited by a theological emphasis and the habit of generations, did not include the variety of fields or permit the depth of investigation that existed at colleges where new areas of intellectual endeavor and new freedom in organizing courses of study had been offered to students. Partly on this account student energies focused less upon learning, indeed less upon the whole college, than upon extracurricular activities, "side shows" Wilson was to call them. Nevertheless Princeton enjoyed a rich reputation for past achievement, the devotion of a prosperous alumni, the attendance of their potentially influential sons, and the respect of the community of educated men. Futhermore, in electing Wilson president, the trustees selected a spokesman of the dissidents who had forced the few reforms of his predecessor's regime. Wilson was clearly the preferred candidate of the faculty. Auspiciously appointed, challenged by his task, he began at once to make Prinecton what his vision of a university told him Princeton had to be.

Princeton, he believed, had to become a place from which young men would go out equipped in every way he valued to serve the nation. It had, therefore, to be an outstanding home not only of scholarship but also of experience larger than scholarship. "There is an ideal at the heart of everything American," Wilson asserted, "and the ideal at the heart of the American university is intellectual training, the awakening of the whole man, the thorough introduction of the student to the life of America and of the modern world . . . The college . . . therefore, is a place intended . . . not for intellectual discipline and enlightenment only, but also for moral and spiritual discipline and enlightenment."

In making Princeton such a college he kept in mind two models. One was the Hopkins seminar, the periodic meeting of small groups of graduate students and their mentors for a critical exchange of ideas, which inspired him to provide for Princeton undergraduates a comparable experience. He resolved to do this without abandoning instruction in the Christian tradition that had always been the core of the college's curriculum. This was the tradition also of Oxford and Cambridge, those wombs of British statesmen, Wilson's heroes. He wished with appropriate modifications to graft the spirit of the English universities upon Princeton, his mother-presumptive of American leadership. His plans entailed the reorganization of the administration, the curriculum, ultimately the physical environment of the college, the raising and spending of over twelve million dollars, at that time an unprecedented sum. He needed not just the approval but the continuing cooperation of the alumni — his constituents; the faculty — his Commons; and the trustees — his Lords, and in this case his masters. But he had been preparing to preside in such a pass, and for a time his ministry was brilliant.

During the three years after his inauguration Wilson completed reforms at Princeton that influenced the whole of American higher education. Drawing upon the ideas of those of his colleagues who since 1901 had been urging scholastic reform, consulting constantly with them, whetting and guiding the sentiments their agitation engendered, he gave inspiration and direction to the work of his faculty committees and primed the Princeton environment to welcome their recommendations. In this manner he created what is now the system of organization of most universities, the grouping of related departments in several differentiated divisions. This facilitated the operation of a new curriculum which focalized student learning while preserving a degree of common educational experience and avoiding the confusion of an indiscriminate elective system. Fewer but more rigorous courses were required each year. Lowerclassmen continued to study a common program; upperclassmen concentrated most of their time on the work of one division and one of its departments. Most American colleges have since copied this arrangement. The average undergraduate has come to cap his education by exploring a particular field of concentration. Furthermore, the recent emphasis on general education reflects the same concern that stimulated Wilson to expose all students to a common introductory program and to a further experience in some area other than their specialty.

The core he prescribed, moreover, like many current experiments, purposed to convey "moral and spiritual enlightenment."

Wilson's revised administration and curriculum, striking innovations in themselves, provided a structure for and were in turn enhanced by his dearest invention, the preceptorial system. He developed this plan to rid Princeton of the educational practice that required students only to record and recall the data contained in textbooks and lectures. He proposed to appoint as assistant professors a group of young men as vigorous as Hopkins scholars, as cultivated as Oxford dons, to serve as "the companions and coaches and guides" of student reading in each department. These preceptors were to bring zest to the reorganized curriculum, to instill the spirit of learning in undergraduate life, to "transform the place from a place where there are youngsters doing tasks to a place where there are men doing thinking." Although the alumni did not, as Wilson hoped they would, at once endow the preceptorial system, they did supply sufficient funds for its beginning. With modifications it has persisted at Princeton, a few wealthy institutions have adopted equivalent plans, and many others have arranged to provide students with the opportunity to work personally with some of their instructors.

The success of the reforms at Princeton owed much to Wilson. Exercising remarkable judgment, he recruited an outstanding staff. His own persuasive enthusiasm and the excitement attending his bold departures attracted to Princeton not only the preceptors but also more mature scholars. A sense of adventure, a spirit of high purpose pervaded the college, making higher standards a challenge rather than a burden for most students, delighting alumni.

Princeton's most valuable asset, they told each other with satisfaction, was Woodrow Wilson. For the inspired faculty this was the finest hour of long seasons of teaching still to come. "Bliss it was," Wilson's young men — grown old — have recalled, "in that dawn to be alive."

So indeed it must have been; but college professors, like other men, could not remain for long euphoric. Conflicts over salary and rank, over building and research funds created factions. Courageous, experimental leadership took the willing to a glad summit but left behind a waspish corps to whom change denied accustomed status. While he built, Wilson had to deny this man's request, discharge that man's friend. Sooner or later the buoyancy that Wilson had brought to Princeton was bound to be disturbed. As it happened, Wilson himself, pressing for further change to consummate his program, precipitated trouble.

Determined as ever to "push on," conscious of his unparalleled popularity and success, Wilson in December, 1906, recommended a sweeping reform of the physical arrangement and social life of the college. Without warning or discussion, he proposed the abolition of upper-class eating clubs — the Princeton equivalent of fraternities. By combining the clubhouses with new construction, he wished to build quadrangles where groups of students from each of the classes and some resident faculty members would live and eat together. Once again he had in mind the colleges at Oxford and Cambridge, the models for the reorganizations of Harvard and Yale in later years. Just as the preceptorial system integrated and invigorated the intellectual life of the Princeton students, so were the quadrangles to coordinate and revitalize their social life.

Incontestably the eating clubs were undemocratic.

Those sorry juniors and seniors who made no club languished apart from college life. The elect became the willing captives of the small fraternity and the indulgent luxury of the particular club to which they belonged. Birth, wealth, and manner rather than merit governed the selection of clubmen and the differentiation of membership between the right and the not-so-right clubs — in all, an unhappy situation worsened by the capacity of youth for unintended cruelty. But Wilson did not yet choose to champion democracy at Princeton. His purpose, as he saw it, was much more idealistic.

He intended to provide "in the midst of play" a "constant consciousness" of what Princeton meant, to enrich student leisure with interests study created, thereby to intellectualize, elevate, and unify the life of the college. Under existing conditions, deliberately neglecting learning, boys spent their energies on conforming to the mores or serving the interests of their fraternities. Believing as he did that a university should be primarily an intellectual community, Wilson could not countenance the inversion of values he saw around him. Cherishing Princeton not just as an institution but also as a corporate embodiment of a way of life, he resented the divisive dispersion of loyalties the clubs demanded. Within the quadrangles, he judged, faculty and students, upperclassmen and lowerclassmen would achieve together a wholeness of interest and purpose that would enlist the young men of Princeton and the college itself in the service of the nation.

This noble end included incidentally egalitarian reform, a matter of relative indifference to Wilson but of importance to Princeton men. Perhaps because he realized this, he did not consult or even inform most of the faculty or any of the alumni before he asked the board of trustees to approve his plan for the social coordination of the university. Acceding to his request, the board in June, 1907, authorized him to work out the details with the clubs and others concerned. Wilson then published his report on the quadrangle proposal.

At once a fight began within the surprised faculty. When several prominent professors expressed opposition to the plan and distress at Wilson's peremptory method of presenting it, he replied that they would have the chance to discuss fully the ways in which change was to be effected. The basis of his program, however, he regarded as an accomplished fact. Later he addressed the faculty, rendering a memorable explanation of his purpose. But by this time his audience was restless. His closest friend voted against the quads, for which Wilson never forgave him. Among Wilson's other opponents, some were permanently alienated by his tactics, some at least disenchanted. Others found in the quad fight occasion to release animosities or exploit ambitions earlier accumulated. The articulate opposition of a considerable minority of the faculty naturally disturbed the trustees. But it was the overwhelming sentiment of the alumni, who throughout the summer had registered their persistent attachment to the clubs, that persuaded the trustees in October to withdraw their approval of the plan for social coordination.

At the same time the board, hoping to mitigate Wilson's disppointment, voted to permit him to continue to agitate the issue. This was a mistake, for it left Wilson sufficiently despondent to contemplate resigning but sufficiently angered to prefer vindication. A major defeat, he knew, ordinarily provoked the prime minister to resign, but influenced by his friends and by his own ambition, Wilson decided instead to remain in office while he took his case to his constituency. No more than he had during the summer, however, did the president now tolerate suggestions of compromise. Had he agreed simply to reform the clubs, he could have had the support of almost his entire faculty and of the board. But to reform the clubs was precisely what Wilson did not want, for it would have eliminated a telling argument for the quads; and anything less than quads, he insisted, vitiated his entire educational program. Strategically he could not base his case on democracy; moreover, as he explained to those trustees who urged him to do so, he did not consider democracy the issue. But the issue he defined and took with increasing fervor to the alumni again failed to reach them. Worse still, Wilson's intransigence and that of his allies, generating as it did an equally stubborn resistance, divided the faculty into two sullen groups.

Early in 1908 the question of the quadrangles was closed. A committee previously appointed by the trustees reported after investigation that the clubs, on the whole forces for good in student life, encouraged morality and did not discourage study. Now completely defeated, Wilson was for a time exhausted, dispirited; forever he dropped the issue. According to the principles of leadership he himself had formulated, he never should have raised it or pursued it as he did. Underestimating the force of tradition, which he ordinarily valued, he had neglected accurately to measure the opinion of his constituency or adequately to educate it. He had "pushed on" too soon, relied too much upon himself and his own insights and definitions, misinterpreted resistance as a selfish force which confirmed the merit of his own ideal. In varying degrees overconfidence and impatience spoiled his talents for perception and persuasion. So too did his urge to command. "As long as I am president of Princeton," Wilson in an unguarded moment once told a trustee, "I propose to dictate the architectural policy of the university." He could have said this of any policy. His insistence on his way delayed the democratization of student life. It also cost him loyalties he was about to need to resist a stronger and more genuine challenge to his power.

Foremost of Wilson's opponents during the quadrangle fight was Andrew Fleming West, since 1883 a professor of classics, a scholarly, ambitious, dour man. The leading spirit in the movement to establish a graduate school at Princeton, West had been elected dean of that school when the trustees authorized it in 1900. They then gave him broad control over personnel and policy matters. Responsible to the board and theoretically to the president, West in fact had an empire of his own. He was as jealous of his power and its aggrandizement as Wilson was incapable of tolerating its continuing existence.

For a time, however, they lived in uneasy peace. Wilson in 1902 wrote a preface endorsing the dean's report on the development of a fellowship, faculty, and building program. West in turn supported Wilson's first reforms, even though the drive for funds for the preceptorial system postponed solicitation for the graduate school. Yet there were differences. Before he wrote the preface for West, Wilson made it clear that he wanted the graduate school to be coordinated closely with the college and located in the heart of the campus — objectives at variance with West's plans. West in 1905 opened a temporary residence for graduate students at Merwick, a house off campus. Continuing to consult his own purpose, he sensed the president's hostility. The dean was prepared, therefore, in 1906 to accept an offer to become president of the Massachusetts Institute of Technology. As he explained to the Princeton trustees, he felt that he was not getting along with Wilson. But Wilson, silent while the board discussed his rival's future, signed a strong statement requesting West to remain. Perhaps Wilson was still unable to admit even to himself his incapacity to share power at Princeton. Perhaps he believed that his growing popularity would permit him to discipline West, whose ability to raise money Princeton needed. In any case he erred. Remaining, West interpreted the statement of the president and board as assurance of support.

The war between president and dean, destined to be a long one, began over the quads. Astonished by the publication of Wilson's plan, resenting his method and his objective, West was especially disturbed because the construction of the quads again would have postponed solicitation for the graduate school. This, the dean believed, was a breach of faith. Commander of the faculty's resistance, he enjoyed the president's defeat. The bitterness of that defeat and the advice of those new professors who considered West a dilettante spurred Wilson to retaliate. In March, 1908, the trustees accepted Wilson's decision to build the graduate school on campus at the site of Prospect, the president's residence. Early in 1909 Wilson persuaded the board to reorganize the graduate school, vesting most of West's authority in a faculty committee which the president arranged to have his friends control.

The dogged dean, however, also had friends. From one of these, William C. Procter, he obtained a $500,000 gift for the construction of the graduate school on the condition that the school be built off campus. The struggle for power now turned upon a question of geography. The faculty, already split by the quad fight, again took unyielding

sides, most of them with Wilson. The alumni, less enthusiastic about their president than they had been, by and
large preferred half a million dollars. Wilson could not
persuade Procter to change the stipulations West had arranged, nor would the president explain to the trustees
that the location of the school was not the real issue. In
October, 1909, by a divided vote the board accepted
Procter's gift and chose the golf course as the site for building. West had won the battle.

But not the war. On Christmas Day in a letter to the
trustees Wilson redefined the issue, this time with candor.
What concerned him, he admitted, was power and, of
course, morality. Endowment previously accumulated
could not, he averred, be used in Procter's way. More important, the faculty had lost confidence in West. "Nothing
administered by him," the president insisted, "can now
succeed." Most important, Wilson could interpret the acceptance of the Procter gift and golf course site only as
repudiation of his leadership. The board's vote wrested
from him guidance of education at the university, placing
it in the hands of men of money. Either the gift was to be
declined or he would resign.

At a troubled session in January, 1910, Wilson forced
the matter further. The graduate school, he confessed,
could succeed anywhere in the country if its ideals were
sound. West's ideals were unsound. The dean put luxury
above scholarship, the graduate school above the university. Reminded that he had endorsed West's program in
1902, Wilson maintained that he had not read the dean's
report before writing the preface. This wriggling convinced one trustee that Wilson should leave Princeton.
Several others concluded that he should not have his way
about the Procter gift. But while the board was still un-

decided, Procter in February withdrew his offer, acknowl-
edging that Wilson's attitude was the main cause of his
change of mind. Four days later a committee of the board
reported against the golf course site, a decision simplified
by Procter's action. Wilson had won a battle.

But the enemy was not his. Wilson had irrevocably estranged many of his faculty and a substantial minority of
the trustees. When he sought immediately after his victory to oust West completely, his undisguised desire for
vengeance shocked even his friends. In April the trustees
refused his request to refer the entire question of the graduate school to the faculty, where doubtless Wilson's views
would have prevailed. West's lines were holding.

Wilson now resolved to use an extraordinary tactic. He
would let the people decide, the American people whom
Princeton was built to serve. Speaking to the Pittsburgh
alumni two days after the board declined his request,
frustrated, clearly angry, Wilson let himself go. Since
Princeton was "intended for the service of the country,"
it was "by the requirements of the country that it will be
measured," he began. But privately endowed universities,
oversolicitous of the support of the wealthy, consequently
neglecting the people, were losing the esteem in which
they were held. The college had therefore to "become sat-
urated in the same sympathies as the common people."
What the people wanted, he went on, were leaders to help
them accomplish "their moral regeneration." Failing this,
America, losing "self-possession," would "stagger like
France through fields of blood."

Wilson had aggressively stated his familiar convictions
that democracy was a moral problem requiring sympathetic and adroit leadership for its solution. He now
made a strange equation between this belief, his for many

years, and the controversy at Princeton. Would America, he asked, tolerate the seclusion of graduate students? It could not, for democracy was at stake. Characteristically, he moralized and personalized his case. He made West a satanic figure, propagating evil, challenging the national being by enlisting wealth to give to special privilege the direction of Princeton's destiny.

While Wilson waited for his message to register, he rejected a compromise the trustees proposed. This would have given control of graduate school policy to a faculty committee, built the school on the golf course, and left to West only the role of resident master. But Wilson would not suffer even this solution. And as in the case of the quads, his inflexibility proved expensive.

Dean West, never idle while Wilson contrived, had his turn in May when one Isaac C. Wyman of Massachusetts died. Wyman's will named his old friend Andrew West as an executor and included a bequest, designed by the dean, of several million dollars to endow at Princeton a graduate school patterned precisely on West's plans. The bequest was, as Wilson realized, too important to Princeton, too generous to be refused. He accepted the money, agreed that under the conditions of the will West had to continue as dean, and also accepted Procter's renewal of his offer. West had triumphed.

Wilson's acceptance of the Wyman gift involved considerations of power, personality, morality and democracy which, by his own previous definitions, imperiously suggested his only course. A prime minister whose program completely failed could only resign. A president who surrendered to what he considered snobbery and dilettantism could no longer be of use to his university. Wilson, however, did not at once resign. He lingered until September, when he accepted the Democratic nomination for governor of New Jersey. Without awaiting the outcome of his campaign, but not without relief, the trustees accepted his resignation.

At Princeton Wilson seemed to have mastered the rules for reducing a great empire to a small one. Working as he did during his first years there in an environment prepared to accept his leadership, he exercised extraordinary talents of persuasion, fulfilling thereby the promises which since boyhood he had been making to himself. But in his later years, taxing his environment beyond its immediate tolerances, he permitted his temperament to dull his discernment of men and situations. The nobility he ascribed to his purposes precluded the tactical resilience without which the politics of persuasion could not work. Long before he came to Princeton, after all, long before he encountered opposition there, all issues were for him primarily moral and personal. Given his manner of thought and his intensity of purpose, resistance was bound to make him an obdurate, pertinacious foe. This finally cost Princeton dearly and cost Wilson much of the credit that his magnificent first achievements had earned him. The larger significance of his experience at Princeton no one could then know. He had lived in microcosm there the pattern that would characterize his public career. He had revealed the strengths and the weaknesses of his intelligence and his temperament.

Yet Wilson's star in September, 1910, had not reached its zenith. He had at Princeton a first experience in a tough fight and, though he lost, he showed a durable pugnacity. Both his accomplishments and his contests, furthermore, caught the attention of those trustees of the Democratic party who were looking for a safe man of prominence to bring prestige and victory to their ticket. Ever mindful of such a role, ever faithful to the tenets of his ingrown Democratic faith, Wilson had been using his platform as president of Princeton to sample the responses of the larger environment of American politics. Indeed, his address to the Pittsburgh alumni may have been designed primarily to influence an electorate interested in democracy and a party elite interested in achieving democracy by moral regeneration rather than by social or economic reform. Surely his defeat at Princeton hurt Wilson, but surely also he had never been content with academic life. It was less, perhaps, defeat than aspiration that made him welcome his nomination for the governorship of New Jersey.

III

Giant Steps
1910–1912

COLONEL GEORGE B. M. HARVEY generally knew just what he wanted. His was the first, the incomparable, smoke-filled room where in 1920 the nomination of Warren Harding was arranged. But long before Harding invented the word "normalcy," Harvey had apotheosized the concepts that word contained; and long before 1920, the colonel had assumed the satisfying role of kingmaker. In 1906, with a feeling "almost of rapture," Harvey proposed to the diners at the Lotus Club that Woodrow Wilson should be nominated for President of the United States. The colonel at this time was editor of the *North American Review* and *Harper's Weekly* (his military title was exclusively decorative), an associate of those New York Democrats who had maximized beyond their happiest expectations the profits in public utilities, and a friendly debtor of J. Pierpont Morgan — then almost lord of creation. Men such as these, disturbed equally by the Republicanism of Theodore Roosevelt and the Democracy of William Jennings Bryan, took interest in Harvey's nominating message, which the colonel's periodicals repeated.

The suggestion also pleased Wilson. Nothing, he protested publicly, was further from his thoughts than the possibility of "holding high political office." Privately, however, he confessed a growing impatience with the "minor statesmanship" of education. For the enlightenment of those who took the colonel seriously, including the editor of the New York *Sun*, Wilson composed a credo that attested to his safety. He was willing in 1907 to let the New Jersey Democrats contemplate endorsing him for the Senate; he rather enjoyed speculation about his selection as a national candidate in 1908. As his troubles grew at Princeton, he invited national attention. He also spoke more and more on public issues. As always, he intended that his phrasings of his faiths enthrall a widening audience.

His speeches, Wilson explained, expressed "views which would hold liberal and reforming programmes to conservative . . . lines of action." The national government, he believed, should not directly regulate corporations, for this violated the rights of states and threatened the rights of individuals. Big business, he acknowledged, had come to stay, bringing with it some evils. But these, he thought, were the evils spawned by sinful men. He would pass laws against business sin and punish the transgressors. He would also preach to them a new morality — all this in contrast to Roosevelt's "imprudent willfulness" and Bryan's "foolish and dangerous . . . beliefs." Unlike Bryan, he opposed labor unions, arguing that they impaired the individual laborer's freedom to contract with his corporate employer. Unlike Roosevelt, he failed to understand that not bad men but the attributes of industrial growth created conditions of competition and consolidation that necessitated federal intercession. "You cannot scorch the abuse," Wilson maintained, "but you can consume men by merely exposing them to . . . moral fire." "Scores of business men," he insisted, had "become conscious" of indulging in practices which "they now see to have been immoral." "Capital must give over its too great preoccupation with . . . making those who control it individually rich and must . . . serve the interests of the people as a whole." But because "excess of government is the very antithesis of liberty," he would have no "discretionary control" by the federal executive. Instead businessmen would control themselves. Even banking, he believed, was "founded on a moral basis and not on a financial basis." It was therefore the duty of the banker to avoid "class spirit," "to be intelligent, thoughtful, patriotic," to make loans to the small and weak as well as the large and strong. To straighten out the world of business and finance, Wilson yearned for "some great orator who could go about and make men drunk with his spirit of self-sacrifice."

These observations touched the moral sense of men of wealth without endangering their purses. They knew how difficult it was, no matter what the law, for courts to get evidence of personal rather than corporate misconduct, how reluctant were juries to convict the respectable for circumventing the regulations of the market place. They had learned that the chimera of states' rights protected masters of industry as it had once protected masters of slaves. They were aware, then, that Wilson was creating a diversion useful to them, for the immediate challenge to their purse and power lay in the executive authority of the federal government.

Colonel Harvey had struck it rich. There were plenty of men of his kind, inured to preaching, ready to finance and publicize his candidate. Too wise to rely upon pub-

licity alone, Harvey had also begun to sell his plans for
Woodrow Wilson to the dominant figure in the Democratic party in New Jersey, James Smith, Jr., a former
United States Senator, celebrated largely for his logroll-
ing. Smith presided over the coalition of local bosses who
had fallen into the easy habits of profiting from arrangements with privileged corporations, distributing a limited
largess to the unlettered and indigent of the north Jersey
cities, and losing state elections to their more genteel
but otherwise indistinguishable Republican counterparts.
An Irish immigrant, self-made, self-conscious, carefully
groomed over every inch of his corpulence, Smith knew
he had reached the promised land of politics, but he
hoped also to enter its temple. He had a hankering to
make a President and a hunger to return to the Senate. He
therefore appreciated Harvey's candidate. Here was a man
with a pedigree, something Jersey Democrats had long
conspicuously lacked, a national figure whose perorations
sounded liberal but also safe, a possible governor who
might be made much more.

Wilson, defeated at Princeton, let his old ambitions
swell. Watching Theodore Roosevelt, he had come to recognize the power of the Presidency. Observing politics in
1910, he realized that the growing division between insurgent and standpat Republicans might hand the Democrats a national victory in 1912. "The question of my
nomination for the governorship," he wrote a Princeton
friend in June of 1910, "is the mere preliminary of a plan
to nominate me in 1912 for the presidency." "Representative politicians" in the Middle West, he reported,
were urging Smith to fix his future. Nor was Wilson passive. If elected, he had let Smith know, he would not fight
the organization. He would not seek the nomination but

he would accept it. This was enough for Smith, who prepared to have the Democratic convention name Wilson
with spontaneous enthusiasm. The candidate-to-be discovered to his irritation that he had some rivals. Smith
took care of them. "This is what I was meant for, any-
how," Wilson mused, "this rough and tumble of the political arena. My instinct all turns that way."

The "rough and tumble," such as it was, arose because
the liberal Democrats considered Wilson the organization's puppet. His writings, they observed, evidenced his
enmity toward workingmen and his prejudices against
immigrants, of whom there were many in north Jersey.
But the ordinary beneficiary of the city machine cared less
about Wilson's prejudices than about the generosity of
the local bosses, who, as one of them explained, were concerned only with selecting a winning candidate. Money,
favor, habit worked for Wilson. The liberals, weak at best,
divided among themselves, could not keep Smith from
controlling the convention. He let them write a platform
that might command the enthusiasm of the electorate,
then increasingly of a progressive point of view. He let
them spend their energies demonstrating for their candidates. But he had the convention nominate his candidate
on the first ballot.

The day was still young, the victorious and the dispirited alike about to leave, when the clerk announced
that Wilson was on his way to address them. This en-
trance Harvey had arranged. Most of the delegates remained, some few enthusiastic, some skeptical, most simply curious. Many of them, after all, had never seen a
Princeton president.

As he walked upon the stage of the Taylor Opera House
in Trenton to accept his nomination, Wilson accepted

also a way of life that was to command his extraordinary
capacity for dedication and to compel his unusually steady
mind to unprecedented innovation. As an outside influence on politics he had for twenty years marked time,
turning an emphasis, modifying a point, but never changing much his youthful formulations. Now he had to seek
and win office, a process which, as he had himself explained, involved at once the reading and the writing of
the public's wants. He had to maintain some electric identity between his intuitive self and the elusive consensus
that is the resultant of conflicting political attitudes. Now
in Trenton he began for several sunny seasons with rich
results to bend his will to those he needed. They may have
needed him.

Sure of the organization, Wilson won the liberals at the
Taylor Opera House. "I did not seek this nomination," he
announced. "I shall enter . . . office . . . with absolutely
no pledges of any kind to prevent me from serving the
people." If few delegates believed this, the progressives
were at least glad to hear it. Their pleasure grew as Wilson praised their platform and pledged the reconstruction
of New Jersey's economic, political and moral order. His
words gave to his late opponents, beaten but not rebellious, the excuse they needed to continue being Democrats. They cheered. To this the organization had no objection.

Wilson quickly learned that he had to conduct a campaign pledged to reform. In New Jersey, as in the nation,
the spirit of change had been swelling for a decade. Reformers in both parties, fighting corrupt machines and
corrupting corporations, had waged successful battles to
exact a fair share of taxation from railways and public
utilities, to supervise some of their practices, to establish a

foundation for the use of direct primaries, and to extend civil service. By 1910 the comfortable middle class that resided in New Jersey's expanding suburbs had come to demand further laws calculated to reduce boss rule in the cities, extend direct primaries, and regulate the rates for gas, electricity and commutation tickets. Labor had come to expect legislation establishing the eight-hour day and an equitable employers' liability system.

Although the platforms of both parties spoke these objectives fair, although the Republicans nominated a candidate with a record of cautious progressivism, Wilson at first discussed only the high cost of living, the new and unpopular Republican protective tariff, the indispensability of morality in government. But these emphases, he soon realized, failed to stir the electorate. He began therefore on the last day of September to deal specifically with local issues. During the next month, working from his platform, advised by experienced New Jersey Democrats, he advocated laws to curb the trusts, to give the Public Service Commission authority to fix rates, to prevent corrupt practices, to permit the popular election of United States Senators. "I am," he insisted, "and always have been an insurgent."

This, of course, was nonsense, though Wilson shared some attitudes then fashionable with the left. For several years before his nomination he had written earnestly about the need for making local government responsible and efficient. Like the suburban voters whose support he now solicited, he had had a genuine desire to minimize the brogue in city politics. Like them, he had wished their Wall Street neighbors would behave. But these pieties were completely compatible with Wilson's persisting conservatism.

During the campaign he modified his conservatism on only two points. First, adopting a new vocabulary, he identified himself, as he never had before, with change. Second, urging that a commission set rail and utilities rates, he advocated at last regulation by direct, continuous administrative action. This was an important party issue. The Republicans, handicapped by their record on the matter, were further penalized by their candidate's promise to follow rather than to lead the legislature. Because the railroads, with incredibly bad timing, had just raised their local rates, the commuters displayed an extraordinary sensitivity to the question of regulation. Significantly, Wilson carried the traditionally Republican suburbs in 1910, but never again.

Wilson's canvass reached its dramatic climax late in October, when he replied in a public letter to a series of questions asked by George L. Record, the most celebrated Republican progressive in the state. Record's questions covered the whole spectrum of outstanding issues. Wilson's response not only repeated the points his speeches had been making but also pledged him to extend direct primaries beyond the limits the organization had defined in the platform and to champion workingmen's compensation. Record asked how Wilson would treat the Smith machine. "I shall not," Wilson wrote, "either in the matter of appointments to office or assent to legislation . . . submit to the dictation of any person or persons, special interest or organization . . . I regard myself as pledged to the regeneration of the Democratic party."

Saluted as it was by independent editors and voters, Wilson's reply helped his cause. Other conditions also counted heavily in his favor. While he spoke regeneration to the polite, his fellows on the stump amused larger audiences with "give 'em hell" addresses, and the organization reached the mass of voters in its effective ways. The powerful little boss of Jersey City, in other years often at odds with Smith, in 1910 imposed upon his many faithful an unprecedented unanimity for Wilson. The chairman of the state committee, Smith's son-in-law, James Nugent, employed a discriminating combination of funds, warnings and assurances to activate the local Democratic leaders who, like him, had tired of defeat. Unity of purpose pervaded the Democratic wards. In contrast, the Republicans suffered from the growing national division between their conservative and liberal factions and from the widespread resentment toward the tariff that Wilson so continually censured. All this helped Wilson poll the second largest plurality in the history of the state.

Of the many Democratic victories in 1910, Wilson's was the most compelling. Harvey and his friends gained confidence; Smith, prominence — or so he hoped. At the same time, built as he was, Wilson believed in the principles of his campaign as soon as he began to preach them. Of his sincerity, though he moved with the wind, there can be no doubt. His campaign had pleased Democrats who sought a liberal candidate for 1912 and independent voters in New Jersey who expected a reform administration right away. Consequently, just as the nation came to watch him, he served two sets of masters, those who had arranged his nomination and those who believed they had elected him. Almost at once both claimed reward.

Wilson's creditors clashed over the election of a United States Senator. This function then still fell to the state legislature, where, for the first time in many years, the Democrats had just won a majority of the seats. James Smith, Jr., considered himself entitled to the office which his party was to bestow. Supported as he was by his own friends and by the Jersey City machine, he also thought that he commanded the necessary votes. The progressive Democrats had other plans. Always opposed to Smith, they had in 1910 a special, moral issue. A state law permitted voters to register a preference for candidates for the Senate. Although the law did not bind the legislature, although only a small fraction of Democrats had chosen to indicate a preference, the progressives maintained that the victor in the preferential vote deserved to represent the state in Washington. The principle of popular election of senators, they argued, a principle endorsed by the platform and by Wilson, was at stake. They were particularly outraged because Smith, by refusing to register for the preferential contest, had displayed his disdain for the processes they valued. Both sides solicited help from Wilson.

The governor-elect understood that neutrality was out of the question. If he did not assist the progressives, they had warned him, he would lose their support for his program, support he needed to be an effective governor and an attractive presidential candidate. Were he, however, to oppose Smith, he would incur the antagonism of the organization and distress those "representative politicians" who had blessed his aspirations. Furthermore, the victor in the preferential contest, the darling of the liberals, was James Martine, a Bryan Democrat who had brought only a comic, common touch to his continual, unsuccessful, fatuous campaigns for offices in the state. "Farmer Jim" was scarcely Wilson's kind of man. But with his eyes upon his future, yet not without courage, Wilson made Martine his candidate. Attributing his election to the governorship to the support of progressives, he explained to George

Harvey that Smith was "intolerable" to those "very people." The problem, Wilson went on, was national; if independents lost confidence in him, they would turn again to Theodore Roosevelt. He hoped therefore that Smith, of whom he had a "high opinion," would withdraw; otherwise he "would have to fight him." Smith bridled at this warning. The fight was on.

Almost immediately Wilson formed a new opinion of Smith. Drawing upon the large stock of progressive attitudes toward the ex-senator, he made him, as once he had made West, an incarnation of evil, a symbol of corruption, subservience to wealth, contempt for popular opinion. He persuaded himself, but never Smith, that Smith had promised not to seek the senatorship. By the end of December Wilson had conferred with almost every Democrat in the legislature, each of whom felt the intensity of manner that accompanied Wilson's dedication to a cause. Especially in public he now emphasized, as he had not to Harvey, the principle of popular elections. In January he went to the people to bring their pressure to bear on wavering assemblymen. "These are our terms," Wilson stated. "War, if you are allied with the enemy. Peace if you are on the . . . side of justice." Smith held only a paper fortress, he declared, and "as in the old Bible stories, the first shout of victorious and irresistible free men causes the stronghold to collapse."

Soft speaking probably proved more effective. When Smith began a whispering campaign intended to show that Wilson hated Catholics, one of Wilson's agents whispered to the Clan-na-Gael that Smith had once voted for a treaty kind to England. Wilson preferred not to think about the large patronage that was to be his to dispense, but his assistants quietly rallied to Martine's cause a number of men whose concern for appointive office was legendary. The death of the Jersey City boss released the legislators from that area from their commitment to Smith. Most of them came over to Martine at the eleventh hour; most of those who did were in time appropriately rewarded. The governor's arsenal was rich, his performance convincing, his mission just. On the legislature's second ballot Martine won election. "I pitied Smith at the last," Wilson claimed. "He wept, they say, as he admitted himself utterly beaten." He also primed his organization to oppose everything the governor attempted.

But during the next three exhilarating months, Wilson led on, "deeply moved," according to his own account, "by the thought of . . . new responsibilities as the . . . champion of the common people." So stimulated, he consulted progressives of both parties about the program he took to his legislature, a program calling for the enactment of those laws which had been the object both of progressive agitation and his campaign. His first test came over the measure reforming the state's primary and election practices. In behalf of this bill Wilson again went to the people, conferred with members of the legislature, even attended the Democratic caucus. The governor's assistants, as they had before, arranged to reward the responsive. These pressures carried the bill through the Democratic assembly; a bipartisan progressive majority saw it through the senate.

So it was also with the rest of the legislation Wilson sponsored: a corrupt-practices act, a law investing the Public Service Commission with power to set rates, a workingmen's compensation law; a law enabling municipalities to adopt the initiative, the referendum, the recall, and the commission form of government. Between Janu-

ary and May, 1911, New Jersey, "the tenderloin state,"
became a model for proponents of reform.

This change, so rapidly effected, brought Wilson a national reputation for courageous leadership. He had
worked hard, refused compromise with the machine,
phrased gracefully the gospel of change. "I wrote the platform," he exulted privately. "I had the measures formulated to my mind, I kept the pressure of opinion constantly on the legislature." "The result," he judged,
"was as complete a victory as has ever been won." The triumph, he implied, was his alone. This assessment, shared
though it was by most casual observers of events in New
Jersey, denied credit to the men who had spent ten years
preparing the environment which Wilson had exploited.
It also overlooked the men who attended to those manipu-
lations Wilson considered beneath his dignity, who built
the new organization without which he could neither govern nor advance his national ambitions.

The construction of the new Democratic order had
commenced with the solicitations of support made for
Martine and accelerated while the legislature met. Wilson, preserving unembarrassed his faith in the persuasive function of the premiership, assigned the predatory
errands to two progressive but politically sophisticated
wardens, the young Irish Democrat he had appointed his
private secretary and the editor of the Trenton *Times*.
Assisted by fellow progressives and by ambitious regulars
restless for larger powers, these two allocated executive
appointments so as to bring to Wilson's side a corps of influential Democrats including a majority of the state committee. Through these men and the day-laborer jobs
which they in turn controlled, Wilson's guardians, after
the legislature recessed, recruited also the essential loyal-

ties of the urban precincts. Their work directly challenged the supremacy of the Smith organization, which Wilson had promised to léave intact. There were hot words. In March, State Chairman Nugent berated Wilson for using patronage to help the primary bill. The indignant governor commanded him to leave his suite. Months later Nugent offered to some officers of the National Guard a toast to Woodrow Wilson, "a liar and an ingrate." Shortly thereafter the Wilson men elected a new chairman of the state committee. They also salted the assembly ticket in 1911 with sufficient of the unregenerate to build their strength in Jersey City. Wilson endorsed these men. He also signed as time went by appointments that won him adherents among the Irish, Jews, Italians, barkeeps. As those who arranged these matters knew, this helped in sections where words failed.

Wilson concentrated his energies on verbalization. Stimulated and convinced by his successful role as champion of change in New Jersey, sensitive to the national spirit that responded to this calling, he pursued his providential star on podiums throughout the country. South and West he castigated privilege, monopoly, protective tariffs. He ventured even to attack the "money trust" by which Pierpont Morgan allegedly controlled America. His new vocabulary, although it rarely dealt with specific recommendations, identified moral regeneration no longer with conservative ways but with the ways of liberal reform. Indeed, Bryan, so recently a dangerous and foolish foe, became now a statesman whose influence deserved solicitation; and the Commoner, aware that Wilson might be a winner, reciprocated with solicitations of his own.

All this forced Harvey to jettison his plans. The election of Martine, the defenestration of Nugent destroyed the image he had erected for the "representative politicians." The reform of New Jersey, the resonance of Wilson's speeches, the rapport with Bryan chilled the ardor of the governor's first moneyed sponsors. When the legislature recessed, most of the original Wilson men had fled to other camps. In the ensuing months the colonel, unable to bring Wilson back to his course, began himself to look for an escape. This left the task of making Woodrow Wilson President to a coterie of amateurs, financed primarily by Wilson's Princeton friends, who from New York attempted to apply throughout the nation the pattern of the Jersey salient: overt appeals to the minds of independents, covert arrangements with amenable professionals. As 1912 began, with less than six months remaining before the national convention, they faced "dark days." Wilson was about to feel the counterthrusts of those he had estranged.

Smith had already taken some revenge by helping the Republicans carry the legislature elected in 1911. During the session of 1912 his allies joined with them in ignoring Wilson's recommendations, exploiting the saturation of the suburbs with reform, and harassing the governor by complaining constantly of his neglect of state affairs. In fact, Wilson campaigned so much that he had little time for executive leadership. Left largely to its own devices, the legislature passed fifty-seven bills he felt obliged to veto. One of these, characteristic of the futile session, provided for the elimination of grade crossings according to a schedule grossly unfair to the railroads. Wilson's veto, inviting as it did the misunderstanding of those who saw in railroads only evil, took courage, but, like the rest of his official errands in 1912, it won him no glory.

Outside of New Jersey there was other trouble. In January, 1912, just before the Jackson Day dinner, the traditional occasion for all Democratic saints to adore each other, the New York *Sun* published a letter Wilson had written in 1907 expressing the hope that something be done "to knock Mr. Bryan once for all into a cocked hat." The timid among Wilson's counselors trembled, but Bryan, at first annoyed, quickly decided that future harmony meant more to him than past disagreements. Wilson, on the advice of his steadier friends, issued no recantation. Instead, addressing the diners, he urged all good Democrats to come to the aid of their party and of mankind, to beat the special interests with "shillalahs . . . of good Irish hickory," and to honor the "steadfast vision . . . the character and the devotion and the preachings of William Jennings Bryan."

"That was splendid," Bryan told him, "splendid."

George Harvey contrived the next crisis. At a luncheon in December Harvey had asked whether the "Wilson-for-President" banner on the masthead of *Harper's Weekly* was hurting the campaign. Rather abruptly, Wilson replied that it did him no good. This brusqueness, several friends suggested to the governor, might have offended Harvey. Wilson therefore wrote a letter of apology to which the colonel sent a cordial answer. But in January, implicitly confirming rumors that there had been a tiff, Harvey told the press that, at Wilson's request, the masthead banner was withdrawm. Although subsequent publication of their correspondence clarified the matter, the impression remained widespread, as Harvey probably intended, that Wilson had again turned on a friend. Wilson's propagandists accused Wall Street of slandering their candidate, but with Smith, Nugent and Harvey all in mind, Democratic politicians could not avoid recalling the dictum of their trade that "an ingrate in politics is no good." There was, after all, a self-righteousness in Wilson that disturbed his relationships with a series of sometime friends.

More disturbing as 1912 wore on were the gains of his opponents for the nomination. The novelty of a professor in politics, the dimensions of his success in New Jersey, the impressions of his early speaking trips had given him some head start. His managers expected to win his native South and much of the insurgent West. During the spring, however, Oscar W. Underwood of Alabama, campaigning on Southern sectionalism, Southern conservatism, and his own bland record, won most of Dixie. Even more upsetting was the boom of Champ Clark of Missouri, Speaker of the House of Representatives, who had long supported agrarian measures, traded favors with fellow party hacks, and attracted voters with his folksy, "Ol' Hound Dawg" ways. Democrats of wealth and power were sure that they could manage Clark, William Randolph Hearst made Clark his darling, and the resistance of the Democratic House of Representatives to the policies of the unpopular President Taft gave Clark a useful platform. Following the lead of the New York *Sun*, the Hearst papers castigated Wilson for having applied for a pension from the Carnegie Fund for the Advancement of Teaching, a subsidy, they claimed, from the enemy of steel workers. Drawing on the anti-Populist, antilabor, anti-immigrant pages of Wilson's *History of the American People*, pages that the governor could not explain away, they provided city machines with effective propaganda for the Ol' Hound Dawg. In state after state Clark carried Democratic primaries. By the end of May it was clear that he would have a majority at the convention.

Through the discouraging winter and spring the Wilson men fought on. The governor traveled South and West again, carrying in his pocket Kipling's "If," cultivating the common touch, doubting all trusts but trusting himself. His publicists attributed each defeat to Wall Street deviltry. His managers displayed willingness to deal with the hard-shell professionals, most of whom nonetheless preferred to deal with Clark. Yet there were important victories — in Pennsylvania, Texas, Wisconsin, half a dozen smaller states, and in New Jersey, where Smith's rough tactics met retaliation just as rough. Although Clark could count on a majority, it would take a two-thirds vote to nominate a candidate, and Wilson's men went into the convention with over one third in their control, enough to block the Speaker at least for several ballots.

The Democratic legions marched to Baltimore ebullient with a sense of impending victory. The Republicans had just retreated from the havoc of Chicago, where Theodore Roosevelt, crying fraud, had left the party, taking with him almost half the delegates and almost all the glamour. For the first time since 1892, the last year of Democratic victory, there was to be a third strong party in the field. The carousing ranks at Baltimore and their calculating captains prepared, therefore, to name not just a candidate but the President.

In the quiet of his summer residence at Sea Girt, New Jersey, Wilson looked on, only superficially contained. Bryan gave him a first chance to do immortal work. Resisting the movement to make Judge Alton B. Parker, a conservative New Yorker, temporary chairman of the convention, Bryan sent identical telegrams to Wilson, Clark and several other candidates requesting each to express his preference for a progressive keynoter. Expecting as he did to lead a harmonious party, Clark hedged in his reply. Wilson's managers in Baltimore, still hoping for Tammany support, advised the governor also to straddle. But Wilson's wife and his secretary, confirming his own preference, insistently disagreed. "You are quite right," Wilson answered Bryan. "The . . . convention is to be a convention of progressives." This unequivocal reply, the only such Bryan received, impressed all liberal delegates and pleased the Commoner, whose influence still was large. So also was his irritation when Clark votes won Parker the temporary chairmanship, a victory in which Bryan thought he saw a coalition between the Tammany Tiger, his ancient foe, and the agents of the Ol' Hound Dawg.

Wilson's managers labored to arrange coalitions of their own. They agreed with the Underwood men to resist any stampede to Clark. They voted to resolve the contest between Illinois' two quarreling factions by seating the delegation of the state boss, who reciprocated by aiding Wilson's cause in other contests. They continued to court Tammany Hall. They organized seventy-five minutes of noise for Wilson — Clark's demonstration had lasted ten minutes less. But the Speaker led on the first ballot and on the tenth, when New York swung to his column, his 536 votes considerably exceeded a majority. Since 1844 every candidate who had won half the votes had gone on to win the nomination.

Wilson at first capitulated. Instructing his managers to release his delegates, he let thoughts of summer travel assuage his discontent. But the urgings of his second in command persuaded him not to concede. And the drama of the fourteenth ballot gave him new hope. It was then that Bryan, following the lead of his fellow Nebraskans, switched his vote to Wilson, explaining sententiously to the convention that he would back no candidate for whom New York was voting. Perhaps he was tilting again with his traditional target, perhaps he intended to help Wilson, perhaps he hoped to prolong a deadlock that would bring the convention once again to him. Always a confused man, Bryan probably did not himself examine his motives, but his action helped stop the drift toward Clark and infuriated the Speaker, who hastened at once to Baltimore. After twenty-six ballots, though Clark still led, he had lost his majority.

During Sunday, June 30, the convention adjourned, officially to honor the Sabbath, actually to let the delegates find some solution to their impasse. Perhaps out of naïveté, perhaps with an instinct for publicity, Wilson informed the press that no bargains could be made in his name. Properly incredulous, his managers spent a fruitful day with the masters of the delegations from Indiana and Illinois. For a price, the Hoosiers learned, their governor and favorite son could have the Wilson votes for the vice-presidential nomination. On Monday's second ballot Indiana switched to Wilson, who then for the first time passed Clark. Illinois' leader, grateful for earlier help from the Wilsonians, hopeful of future favors, moved next. On the forty-third ballot, on Tuesday, Illinois' fifty-eight votes for Wilson gave him a majority. Clark's lines began to break. The Wilsonians urged Underwood's managers to concede. On the forty-sixth ballot Alabama withdrew her man. That did it. Clark's delegates were at once released. At Sea Girt a brass band played "Hail to the Chief."

That march was premature but pertinent. Wilson's nomination, effected as it had been by a coalition of progressive and machine Democrats, permitted his party to avoid factionalism and to offer the electorate a vigorous candidate with a liberal record. There were some small troubles: Champ Clark nursed a sulk and kept it warm; Tammany and its opponents in New York strained briefly before swallowing their local gnats. But no Democrat of reputation cared to miss sharing the probability of power. In contrast, Theodore Roosevelt's new Progressive party had a candidate without an organization, and the Republicans, grass widows for the season, went through the quadrennial rituals with little enthusiasm and less hope.

Wilson and his aides aggressively pursued their advantage. They embraced their preconvention opponents, placed a Clark man on the national committee, conducted a noisy solicitation for one-dollar contributions to the campaign fund but also quietly welcomed large gifts from friendly men of wealth, set up auxiliary headquarters in Chicago to combat Roosevelt in the insurgent Middle West, made calculated appeals for support to Catholics, Jews, Negroes, labor and the foreign-born. These appeals helped sustain the habitual loyalty to the Democracy of much of the urban laboring force. Evoking other loyalties, Bryan swung through the West, spending in Wilson's behalf the full measure of his grandiloquence. With less attention the South stayed safely solid.

All this, essential though it was — indeed, probably controlling — did not relieve Wilson from the challenge of Theodore Roosevelt. Surely the most popular man in America, the Rough Rider had been a great President. He had sponsored important reforms. He had dealt forcefully and dramatically with the heads of the major governments of the world. He had received more publicity, contributed more color, earned more love — and more hate — than any of his contemporaries. Convinced that reactionary trickery had denied him the Republican nomination, he went to the country in 1912 not only with a new party but also with a bold program and a purpose at once vengeful and evangelical.

This program, the New Nationalism, proceeded from Roosevelt's belief, shared by some of the wisest men of his time, that the consolidation of the American economy, an inevitable and salubrious attribute of industrial modernity, necessitated the vigorous exercise by the federal government of broad powers. The efficiency and productivity of big business, Roosevelt held, precluded its atomization, but its power had to be balanced and controlled by the authority of the federal executive. The national government, furthermore, the greatest of all American consolidations, had to promote the welfare of those groups which had not as yet shared adequately the richness of national life. To this end he advocated the use of federal power to promote collective bargaining, ensure workmen's compensation, set wage and working standards, and underwrite health and conservation programs. Besides all this, he advocated woman suffrage, the initiative, the referendum, and the recall of judicial decisions.

Roosevelt was probably more of an issue in himself than was his New Nationalism, but his record and personality, attractive to many voters, alienated others. In his years in office he had had to compromise so often that many could not quite believe him now, others he had offended, still others feared him. So it was that Samuel Gompers, president of the American Federation of Labor, endorsed Wilson even though the Democrats offered labor less than did the Progressives. That most adamant of all insurgents, Senator Robert La Follette of Wisconsin, believing that his own presidential chances had been wrecked by Roosevelt's plotting, remained titularly a Republican in 1912 but worked for Wilson. As Wilson intensified his canvass, some forty thousand — many of them men of parts — joined the Wilson Progressive Republican League.

Not only the need to recruit these men but also his own temperament forced Wilson to abandon his initial, evasive concentration on such hoary Democratic issues as states' rights and tariff reduction. Although less bombastic than Roosevelt, Wilson was just as self-assured, just as devoted to his own precepts, just as much a fighter. As Roosevelt had come gradually over a decade to his New Nationalism, so Wilson for fewer years and over different routes had reshaped his attitudes. Late in August Louis Brandeis, perhaps the most splendid legal intelligence of this century, helped Wilson to organize his thoughts.

An expert on business affairs, an experienced counselor to labor, a veteran of battle with the New Haven Railroad in Massachusetts politics, Brandeis made a cogent case against big business. The powerful corporations that dominated each of several industries, he argued, among themselves controlled credit, raw materials, and markets, preventing competition and protecting what he considered to be their own inefficient administrations, obsolescent plants, and excessive profits on overcapitalized values. The "trusts," too big to be efficient, had corrupted government to gain privilege and protection. He proposed that they be prosecuted and dissolved, that the rules of competition for the future be defined and enforced by the federal government, that credit facilities be erected for little business and new entrepreneurs. Brandeis's data documented Wilson's own nascent theories; Brandeis's dicta provided Wilson with policies much more practicable than that of making all guilt personal; Brandeis's insights inspired Wilson to oppose the New Nationalism with a doctrine of his own, one with an equally engaging title, the New Freedom.

Recognizing that the obligations of government had been increased by modern industrial society, Wilson maintained that these obligations should be of a police nature, involving the making and the enforcing of the rules of economic behavior, eliminating the dangers of big business and with them the need for big government or a Rooseveltian welfare state. He preferred, as he always had, a minimized national authority, a federal system leaving large areas of authority to the states, a society adjusting itself through the competition of determined but decent men. The Rooseveltian way, he averred, would result in "an avowed partnership between the government and the trusts." His alternative, by ensuring a free economy, would preserve free government, avoid decision making by "private understanding and expert testimony," thereby encourage decision making in open parliamentary debate uninhibited by furtive and irresponsible arrangements. "Free men," he postulated, "need no guardians." Indeed, they could not submit to guardians and remain free, for, he maintained, "there are two kinds of corruption — the crude and obvious sort, which consists in direct bribery, and the much subtler, more dangerous, sort, which consists in a corruption of the will."

His difference with Roosevelt was more than that between "regulated competition" and "regulated monopoly." They differed about the nature and obligation of government, the concentration and use of power. Merging Brandeis's political economy with the political theory of his own youth, Wilson made the New Freedom, as he put it himself, "only the old revived and clothed in the un-

conquerable strength of modern America." "Rural Tory-
ism," Roosevelt called it, not without perception. Addressed though it was to twentieth century problems, it
preserved the romantic individualism that Wilson cherished. "In our day the individual has been submerged,"
he lamented, "swallowed up in the . . . great organization"; "there has come about an extraordinary and
very sinister concentration in the control of business in
the country," a concentration especially intolerable because "the masters of the government . . . are the combined capitalists . . . of the United States." Above everything else, therefore, the country needed "a body of laws
which will look after the men who are on the make,"
"the men who are sweating blood to get their foothold in
the world of endeavor."

If Wilson implied the existence of a conspiracy that did
not exist, if he proposed a social order no longer entirely
feasible, he nonetheless understood the aspirations of the
man on the make. He had been and still was, after all,
such a man. But the New Freedom was more than a paean
to mobility. In it Wilson distilled the principles he had
treasured all his life, principles he accepted as articles of
faith, and tempered them with his growing awareness of
national needs and popular sentiments. He struck at once
nostalgic and progressive notes, affirming, as he did, the
accumulated hopes of the farm, of the small town, of middle-class America, the hopes accumulated also in the
folklore of the nation's history. Again and again, as he
campaigned, to make a point he spoke a parable. Such was
the manner of masters of the spirit, and his purpose remained as it had always been: "to express the new spirit
of our politics and restore our politics to their full spirit-

ual vigor again, and our national life . . . [to] its pristine strength and freedom."

This theme won many hearts. Surely it helped Wilson win the election, though his success owed more to Democratic unity and more still to Theodore Roosevelt's independent venture. With the normal Republican vote divided, Wilson needed only 42 per cent of the popular vote to carry all but seven states and win an overwhelming electoral majority. The Democrats, gaining control of both houses of Congress, won a major party victory. More important, perhaps, the combined Democratic, Progressive and Socialist vote signified that change had routed standing pat. Finally, there was personal victory. Without deceit, without bargaining (though his friends had made arrangements in his behalf), without compromising himself, Woodrow Wilson, so recently a despondent, defeated college president, was President-elect of the United States.

Just yesterday George Harvey's hope and hobby, Wilson had walked only with fastidious men, had shared their thoughts, their luxury, their seclusion. Since yesterday he had discarded Harvey and found character in William Jennings Bryan. Since yesterday he had become the leader of the party of mechanics, tradefolk and immigrants. Since yesterday he had defeated the machine of one Irish politician and used the machines of several others, discovering as he did that men without pedigrees nevertheless had human hearts. Since yesterday he had learned a good deal about the needs and ways of government from radicals and learned as much from hard-shell regulars; he had made an astonishing record of chaperoning legislation and winning campaigns; he had even defeated America's hero. Since yesterday he had artfully adjusted to public sentiments while he no less artfully directed them. He had taken giant steps.

And so he came to the destiny he had always sought; came practiced; came with a mandate of a kind; came at a time when men believed that the problems of society could be solved; came with special faith in his pre-destined ability with the help of God to find righteous solutions; came confident that he could bring to pass a golden age, effect a New Freedom whose essence, by his own account, was "a Liberty widened and deepened to match the broadened life of man in modern America, re-storing to him . . . the control of his government, throw-ing wide all gates of lawful enterprise, unfettering his energies, and warming the generous impulses of his heart, a process of release, emancipation, and inspiration, full of a breath of life . . . sweet and wholesome."

I V

"Crown of the Common Theme"

1913-1917

To THE DISMAY of Washington society and Democratic celebrants, Wilson insisted upon an ascetic inauguration. He canceled the traditional inaugural ball. The parade he had to review, but as the carousing faithful passed his stand, his face registered rather more patience than pleasure. He took his gladness in his brief address. The change in government, he said, meant more than a change of party. It indicated a national intention "to cleanse, to reconsider, to restore." This included such specific obligations as reducing the tariff, reforming the currency and banking system, restricting the trusts. But Wilson emphasized that larger duty he ever tried to serve: "to lift everything that concerns our life as a nation to the light that shines from the heartfire of every man's conscience and vision of the right." "This is not a day of triumph," he concluded. "It is a day of dedication. Here muster, not the forces of party, but the forces of humanity. . . . I summon all honest men, all patriotic, all forward-looking men, to my side. God helping me, I will not fail them, if they will but counsel and sustain me!"

These words inspired. Carried away by his own oratory and the exhilaration of his campaign, Wilson dallied with the thought of government by "progressives only." But he knew that in the months to come the Lord and forward-looking men could help him less than could the forces of the party, and he quickly repaired to the role of its responsible leader. He had no real choice. The Democrats enjoyed a large majority in the House of Representatives and a narrow but working control of the Senate. Had Wilson tried government by liberal coalition, he would have alienated more Democrats than he could have won Republicans and Progressives.

Yet the Democratic party, victorious only because the Republicans had divided, was suspect and disorderly. The business community believed the party simply was not fit to rule. The long years of defeat had cultivated among Democrats habits of opposition that impeded the capacity to govern. Southern Bourbons, furthermore, secure in their rotten boroughs, unsympathetic with much their fellows held dear, commanded the senior positions in most of the influential congressional committees. Wilson had a twofold task, twice difficult: to unite his party so that he could use it to legislate and to change his party so that it would mirror the dispositions of a majority of Americans and thereby win their political allegiance.

"Power," Wilson believed, "consists in one's capacity to link his will with the purpose of others, to lead by reason and a gift for cooperation." Yet impatient as he was with small politics, never gregarious, bored by the common, too abstemious and too inconsiderate to distribute the mixings of good fellowship, Wilson was incapable of meeting politicians on their familiar terms. Indeed, he was incapable of communicating a respect for congressmen which he obviously did not feel.

Fortunately, he knew himself. To learn and turn the purpose of his party, he found subordinates who would do what his temperament precluded. He took care to have among his advisers some representatives of each of the party's several factions, some spokesmen also of each of the country's largest interest groups. By granting and withholding favor, they could discipline the wavering to the consensus which the President could discern in the shifting resultants of their advice. It was for them to "counsel and sustain" him, to set with him directions for the party's policies and growth.

A sampling of Wilsonians suggests the versatility of the group. Albert Sidney Burleson, Postmaster General, a former Texas congressman endowed with a provincial pomposity and bucolic sharpness, manipulated Democratic veterans on the Hill, especially Southerners. William Jennings Bryan, appointed Secretary of State, influenced the agrarian left so long devoted to his orotundity. William Gibbs McAdoo, vigorous, ambitious, intelligent Secretary of the Treasury, Wilson's son-in-law to be, was an admired leader of the liberal amateurs who had managed the pre-Baltimore campaign. Secretary of Labor William B. Wilson, though unskilled in politics, had been a union officer respected by his peers. Joseph P. Tumulty, the President's private secretary, a veteran of Jersey City precincts and machine politics, a Roman Catholic of warmth and humor and high spirits, made among the working press and working party a host of good friends for himself and for the administration.

More useful, more influential than any of these was Colonel Edward M. House, the urbane Texan who attached himself to Wilson in 1911 and rapidly became, in Wilson's words, "my second personality . . . my independent self." Feminine in his solicitude for the President, clever, unobtrusive, House accepted no title or office but assumed large responsibilities. Ingratiating himself with the rich and powerful in America and Europe, he communicated his interpretations of their ideas to Wilson and reported his version of the President's ideas to them. "Take my word for it," one observer of the colonel's power and methods remarked, "he can walk on dead leaves and make no more noise than a tiger."

Wilson relied now upon one, now upon another of these counselors. Some of them he permitted an independence of action which he did not always support. Most of them found him unreceptive to unsolicited advice and impeccably precise but impersonally cool in his gratitude. Though by his own account he could not identify himself with the Presidency, he felt and by his manner accentuated the loneliness of that office. While measuring the conflicting demands made upon government, he avoided much of the risk of becoming the unknowing captive of some one man or interest. And he left himself free, as in theory his prime minister had to be, to cooperate personally with the particular congressmen who molded legislation, free also to go directly to the Congress or the people, to solicit the enthusiasm of groups of men by his eloquence — the "reason" in which he had fullest confidence.

Responsible party government and effective executive leadership resulted in the first significant downward revision of the tariff since the Civil War. Wilson called a special session of Congress to fulfill immediately that perennial Democratic pledge, so important in his own thinking, in his recent campaign, and in the expectations of the many Americans disturbed about the high Republican tariff of 1909 and the rising cost of living for which they blamed it. He dramatized the new session, its purpose and his intended role by addressing Congress personally on April 8, 1913. Not since the early years of the republic had any President delivered a message to Congress. Now with a consciousness of his years of preparation and with a mastery of the situation, Wilson explained that he had come to verify the impression that the President was a person, "not a mere department of the Government hailing Congress from some isolated island of jealous power." It was the duty of Congress, he went on, to eliminate the protection from foreign competition behind which even the crudest American combinations could organize monopoly. "The object of the tariff," Wilson held, "must be effective competition." By abolishing artificial advantages, he proposed to put to business the necessity of efficiency.

Wilson had already begun a fruitful cooperation with the Southern chairmen of the congressional committees in which tariff legislation was structured. Adapting tariff bills formulated at the previous session of Congress, the House rapidly completed its task. Only one month after Wilson's address the Democrats passed a bill reducing average ad valorem rates about 11 per cent, adding a number of consumer goods to the free list, and eliminating the protection previously afforded iron and steel and other products of "the trusts." To compensate for the loss in revenue receipts, the bill levied a modest, graduated income tax, a tax legalized just two months earlier by the ratification of the Sixteenth Amendment.

The test of Wilson's leadership and party discipline came in the Senate, where a defection of just three Democrats could have cost the party its majority. Yet five

Democratic senators from sugar and wool producing states would not support the provisions, included by the House at Wilson's insistence, placing sugar and wool on the free list. This created the possibility of the kind of log-rolling that had so often corrupted tariff making. In conference and by letter Wilson urged upon the dissenters his conviction that "no party can ever for any length of time control the Government or serve the people which cannot command the allegiance of its own minority." He won a first victory when the Senate on May 16 voted against holding hearings on the bill. This closed the preferred forum of the lobbyists determined to preserve protection for the interests that employed them. Their potential influence, however, remained large, especially when one of Wilson's converts announced his recommitment to protected wool. The President then appealed to his entire constituency. "The extraordinary exertions" of "industrious" and "insidious" lobbyists, he stated, distorted the public interest. Public opinion, he hoped, would "check and destroy" this "intolerable burden" on government.

After this statement, no Democrat chose to oppose Progressive proposals for the investigation of Wilson's charges and for the divulgence by all senators of their private properties affected by the tariff. These disclosed the existence of energetic lobbies, including a sugar lobby, and the personal interests of sundry senators in divers tariff schedules, including those on sugar and wool. With a refreshed sensitivity to public opinion, the Democratic friends of wool now enlisted with Wilson, leaving the two sugar men alone in their defection. Reunited, the Senate Democrats preserved free sugar and free wool and reduced the general level of rates another 4 per cent. The progressives of all three parties, furthermore, combined to force the President and the Democratic majority to double the maximum surtax on incomes.

The tariff bill, passed in September after the Republicans prolonged debate to delay the rest of Wilson's program, without abandoning protection reduced swollen rates to dimensions consonant with the needs of a viable international trade. A careful though inflexible law, it removed an accumulation of artificial tariff privileges. Although the outbreak of the European war prevented a satisfactory test of the schedules, they were probably the most equitable in modern American history. The new law also made a halting but portentous modification in the tax structure, shifting some of the burden of federal revenue to those most able to bear it, setting a precedent for a further democratization of taxes a few years thereafter, indeed ultimately for deliberately redistributive taxation. A convincing demonstration that the Democrats would govern, a first product of Wilson's leadership, the act brought the President deserved glory. His address to Congress, his statement on the lobbies, advertised his role. His cooperation with congressional leaders, his ability not only to influence congressmen but also to be influenced by them impressed his colleagues. With considerable satisfaction Wilson mused: "I have had the accomplishment of something like this at heart ever since I was a boy." Yet, he admitted: "I am so constituted that . . . I never have a sense of triumph."

Dedicated to the furtherance of his New Freedom, compulsive as ever, undeterred by the heat of a Washington summer, Wilson had already put to the special session of Congress the problem of correcting the country's anachronistic money and banking system. The issue was difficult and divisive. The panic of 1907 had emphasized the inflexibility of currency and the inelasticity of credit, the need to make them responsive to changing seasonal and geographic demands. The events of that panic had also suggested what later investigations documented, the concentration of financial power in the hands of a small group of Eastern bankers responsible only to the admonitions of their individual consciences and collective interests. Indeed in the months before Wilson's election the hearings of the Pujo Committee had focused public attention on the "money trust."

But none of this was news. Southern and Western agrarians had railed for decades against "Wall Street" domination of the national banking system, the inadequacy of public control over currency and finance, the unavailability of agricultural credits. The cheap-money movements of the late nineteenth century had among their objectives the melioration of these conditions. Resisting this, the bankers themselves, increasingly alive to their own problems, especially after 1907 came more and more to urge the need for some central control of the banking system and for a currency not only responsive to, but also in part based upon, the expansion and contraction of commercial paper.

It fell to Wilson to oversee the modification by the Democrats, particularly by the agrarians, of the banking program of conservative interests. The bankers and their Republican friends had proposed the establishment of a central bank, authorized by the government but controlled privately, empowered on its own liability to issue currency based upon both gold and commercial paper. The first Democratic plan, fashioned by the party's right wing and approved by Wilson, altered this proposal by substituting for the central bank a number of district banks supervised by a federal board. To the President's surprise, this alteration failed to satisfy Secretary of the Treasury McAdoo, the chairman of the Senate Committee on Finance, Bryan and his large following, and Louis Brandeis and like-minded liberals. Brandeis's economic arguments and Bryan's political influence particularly impressed Wilson, who came to understand that a considerable minority of his party, in Congress and out, would not support legislation that failed to give the government control of the federal supervising board (the Federal Reserve Board-to-be) and to make bank notes the obligation of the United States. Addressing Congress on June 23, the President called for banking reform permitting businessmen "freedom of enterprise and of individual initiative" — his own persisting first purpose, assuring a sound and responsive currency, preventing concentration "in a few hands of the monetary resources of the country," and placing "control of the system of banking and of issue . . . in the Government itself."

The concessions Wilson had made fell far short of the demands of Southern agrarians in the House of Representatives. They wanted the banking bill to prohibit interlocking directorates, to provide for public control of the regional reserve banks as well as the federal board, to permit reserve banks to discount short-term agricultural paper, and to prevent the use of commercial paper as a basis for issuing currency. Bryan, however, persuaded them to let him mediate their differences with Wilson, who again adjusted to parliamentary necessity. The President conceded the discounting of agricultural notes and promised that later legislation would take care of interlocking directorates. In return the militants accepted the rest of the bill, which the House passed in September.

New problems arose in the Senate, where three crucial Democrats, largely because of piques about matters of patronage, refused at first to support this bill. This permitted the Republicans to force hearings during which the American Bankers' Association and other business groups exerted considerable pressure against the changes to which Wilson had agreed since his inauguration. The President resorted then to the devices of persuasion he had used during the debate on the tariff. To one recalcitrant Democrat he remarked the importance of party discipline. To the son-in-law of another he tendered an important appointment. In a public statement he insisted, perhaps irresponsibly but probably effectively, that Wall Street was attempting to defeat his bill by creating artificial fears of impending panic. Although Senate conservatives managed to increase the percentage of gold reserves required for the issue of bank notes and to reduce the authority of the Federal Reserve Board, the Democrats by December were again sufficiently united to pass the bill.

Just before Christmas, 1913, Wilson signed the Federal Reserve Act, the most significant piece of domestic legislation of his administration. Remedying, as it did, long recognized financial deficiencies without violating the prevailing dicta of sound economists and imaginative financiers, the act gave the United States its first efficient banking and currency system since the time of Andrew Jackson. It fulfilled in every respect the relevant promises in Wilson's campaign and message to Congress. The regulatory authority of the Federal Reserve Board assured a larger degree of government control over banking than had ever existed before. The provisions of the act also per-

mitted a fluidity of currency and credit adequate for the
short-term needs of business and agriculture. Indeed, the
Federal Reserve system facilitated the relatively easy adjustment of American finance to the strains imposed upon
it during World War I. Only after the agonizing experience of the great depression would the representatives of
the American people begin to understand the need for
federal agencies capable, as the reserve system was not, of
sustained long-range, countercyclical activity. In 1913
most Americans of all points of view and parties, impressed alike by the new law and by Wilson's part in de-
vising it, shared the judgment of the Republican New
York *Tribune* that the President's had been "a great ex-
hibition of leadership."

Wilson observed that he had been "successful with the
tariff and currency bills . . . because the people demanded them, and Congress knew it. It was not the pressure from him, but the pressure of the nation back of
him." Yet in interpreting and channelizing that pressure,
he had not only forced the process of legislation but also
earned for himself and his party the admiration of a growing constituency. To complete what he considered his
mandate, to enhance the record before the fall elections
of 1914, to appease that obsessive sense of unrest that always filled him, he had adverted at once to the problem of
regulating industrial combinations. Before presenting this
issue to the regular session of Congress that convened in
January, 1914, he tried to draw together the confusing
strands of his own and his party's thinking.

There was, it developed, a troublesome want of consensus. Like most Democrats, especially those from the
South, Wilson gave first importance to a definition by Congress of precise rules for corporate behavior, rules that

would guide conduct and prevent monopoly. Some Democrats, however, shared the Progressives' preference for referring the regulation of industry to a powerful federal commission. The idea of a commission attracted many businessmen, but they envisioned its function as rather more to counsel a self-regulating industrial community than to assist the antitrust division of the Department of Justice. Indeed, business spokesmen felt that there had been quite enough agitation and reform. Perhaps hoping to forestall further Pujo investigations and further change, the partners of the House of Morgan voluntarily resigned many of their directorates. Nevertheless, the President still harbored his notion of making business guilt personal; the more radical Bryanites remained resolved to destroy the "money trust," limit the size of corporations, tax corporate income, and regulate stock exchanges; and Brandeis, once a leading advocate of limiting size, now considered fair trade laws a more useful protection for small business. He and Bryan, furthermore, wholeheartedly approved the demand of organized labor for the exemption of unions from the antitrust laws, a prospect that worried Wilson and thoroughly alarmed most businessmen.

After weeks of rumination, Wilson addressed Congress on January 20, in the main emphasizing his own views, albeit gently. With the House of Morgan in mind, he asserted that "antagonism between business and Government" had been succeeded by an "atmosphere of accommodation and mutual understanding." "Legislation," he suggested, "is a business of interpretation, not of origination." Interpreting the "best business judgment" to condemn monopoly, he nevertheless recognized the permissibility — though perhaps not the desirability — of large size. Accordingly he proposed not to prohibit holding companies but to prevent their control by interrelated groups. He also asked Congress to create a commission to assist in the difficult process of dissolving corporations found in restraint of trade, possibly also to advise businessmen. With deliberate care he ignored labor. He included among many recommendations his rusty one that penalties for violating the antitrust laws be inflicted upon the offending officers of corporations rather than the corporations themselves. He concentrated, however, on the need for an explicit legislative definition of the meaning of the Sherman Act. Specification of unfair practices, he believed, would dispel uncertainty, guide business activity, encourage healthy competition.

With Wilson's support, the Democratic leadership in the House of Representatives made the party's focal measure the Clayton bill, of which two central provisions forbade interlocking directorates and defined unfair practices. Again with the President's approval, the House Democrats parried labor's demands by agreeing to exempt labor unions (and also farm organizations) from antitrust prosecution when these groups lawfully pursued legitimate aims. The last reservation proved more important than the exemption. A separate bill established an administrative commission not significantly different from the weak Bureau of Corporations, essentially an investigatory body, which it was to replace.

In the Senate, torn by the antithetical purposes of agrarian and conservative Democrats, the party could not exercise its tenuous control. Discipline returned only after Brandeis induced Wilson to reorient policy. Swinging over to the point of view of the Progressive platform, Brandeis helped to draft a bill creating a Federal Trade

Commission, a regulatory agency to prevent the unlawful suppression of competition. In June Wilson began deploying the power and prestige of his office behind this bill. In August Southern Democrats joined their fellows to pass it, but earlier they had combined with the Republicans to attach an amendment providing for broad court review of the commission's orders. Meanwhile the President had abandoned the Clayton bill. Unprotected, it fell victim to a bipartisan conservative amendment modifying the absolute prohibition of interlocking directorates by countenancing those that did not tend to decrease competition — a standard conveniently subject to permissive judicial interpretation. The Senate did add to the bill the statement that labor henceforth was not to be considered an article of commerce, but this humanitarian declaration, celebrated though it was by the unions, had no legal importance. Finally, the Senate let die an administration and House bill providing for the supervision of railway security issues.

The new antitrust laws, Wilson maintained, along with the tariff and banking acts effected his "single purpose . . . to destroy private control and set business free." But the Clayton Act neither destroyed nor freed nor clarified much. Wilson's claim depended upon the future policies of the Federal Trade Commission and opinions of the Supreme Court. These in time belied him. After 1914 the meaning of the antitrust laws remained substantially as uncertain, as controverted as before, and the concentration of industrial power vastly increased. After 1914 labor leaders, who like Wilson whistled in a judicial dark, discovered that the courts considered many strikes restraints of trade. The confusion in Wilson's own thinking, implicit in his earliest speeches on the trust problem, in his New Freedom, in his vacillations during Congress's debate, were not dispelled by advisers, Democrats or otherwise, who were equally confused. Americans, even liberal Americans, could not agree upon how to discipline their burgeoning economy without inhibiting its productivity. Wilson brought Congress to his changing ways, but his objective did not transcend the indecisiveness of his environment.

Yet with the enactment of the antitrust laws, Wilson for a time considered his mission accomplished. So far as domestic legislation was concerned, he had exhausted the stock of ideas he had brought to his office. Prepared as he now was to let businessmen be good, an attitude perhaps fortified by a general business slump, he let those qualities of mind that had once enchanted George Harvey reassert themselves. In this mood he buried as "unwise and unjustifiable" a bill establishing government banks to extend inexpensive, long range credit to farmers; he gave the Constitution a narrow reading to shelve a measure prohibiting child labor.

Changing conditions accentuated Wilson's turn to the right. With the collapse of the Progressive party in the election of 1914, the Republicans made large gains, especially in the East, that substantially reduced the Democratic margin in the House of Representatives. This seemed to some of Wilson's counselors to symbolize an increasingly conservative national temper. The coming of war in Europe at this time dislocated the American economy. Later, particularly during 1916, the possibility that war might end bred fears that European nations would dump their goods in the United States and that European cartels would dominate international trade. The election and the war served, therefore, to confirm Wilson's inclination to reveal his basic faith in the heartfire of the conscience of men of wealth.

He did this variously. His appointments to both the Federal Reserve Board and the Federal Trade Commission gave dominance to men who had an anxious regard for the traditional concerns of business and finance. He permitted the Federal Trade Commission and the Justice Department increasingly to grant indulgences to powerful corporations. In May, 1916, he supported as "a very wise one" a suggestion of the commission that trade and manufacturing associations "be encouraged in every feasible way by the Government." A month later he endorsed a business-sponsored measure, ultimately enacted, permitting cooperation among firms engaged in export trade "to meet more successfully the organized competition . . . in international markets." At the same time he gave his blessing, long denied, to a bill creating a non-partisan, expert tariff commission whose several purposes included the prevention of dumping of unprotected goods in the American market. All in all, the nullification of liberal legislation by conservative administration, the encouragement of trade associations, so effective in restraining competition, the invitation to home-made cartels set a precedent for the kind of business-government relationship that was in the 1920's to become the pattern of normalcy. There inhered in the New Freedom something of the spirit that was, years later, to lead many of its apostles to the Liberty League.

Before Wilson could fully rehabituate himself to a comfortable conservatism, however, political exigencies compelled him to execute a dramatic left-about-face. The Republican gains of 1914 had hurt the Eastern Democrats more than their Southern and Western brethren. In the

Congress that sat during 1915 and 1916, the agrarians therefore had a larger voice in the caucus and on committees. As the presidential election of 1916 approached, furthermore, perceptive Democratic strategists conceded the Northeast. They planned to carry the country by carrying the Middle West and West, where they had to win the votes of former Progressives, who would otherwise return to the Republicans or simply stay home. The needs of the campaign thereby reinforced the predilections of the congressional left. Wilson responded precisely as he had in 1910 and 1912. Believing in party government and in leadership through cooperation and interpretation, he adopted as his own the attitudes politics required.

Now Wilson cultivated social reformers, farmers, and union labor. During the spring of 1916 he used the full powers of his office to combat, in time successfully, the fierce conservative opposition to the confirmation by the Senate of his appointment to the Supreme Court of Louis Brandeis. Reversing his earlier positions, he encouraged the left-wing Democrats, who now passed rural credits and child labor laws. Union labor had won his sympathy during the sanguinary miners' strike in Colorado in 1914; in the summer of 1916 he gave indispensable support to the railroad brotherhoods. Their differences with management threatened to result in a strike that seriously would have hampered movement of war materials to the Allies. Troubled by this prospect, irritated by management's intransigence, Wilson practically ordered Congress to establish the eight-hour day at ten-hour pay on the railroads. The law accomplishing this cost the roads little, for the I.C.C. permitted them an increase in rates, but the brotherhoods felt victorious and union labor saw in Wilson a new champion. Indeed, before the election the Presi-

by 1916 WW dent had moved a long way from his own position of 1912 toward that of Theodore Roosevelt. He had cause to boast that the Democrats had opened their hearts to "the demands of social justice" and "come very near to carrying out the platform of the Progressive Party" as well as their own.

Wilson's first administration effectuated the basic objectives of the progressive movement. Distinguished by its scope rather than its originality, Wilson's achievement would have been impossible had not others laid a political and intellectual foundation for him. The entire program perhaps satisfied the yearnings of the past better than it anticipated the needs of the future. But the product was nevertheless extraordinary. And the process, the welding into legislation of popular aspirations and partisan objectives, of the presidential and the congressional wills, depended always upon Wilson's executive leadership. His was incontestably a magnificent performance.

In Wilson's time and for the future, furthermore, his management of his party had a significance entirely apart from any specific legislation and unrelated to the recondite idealism of his rich eloquence. Just as he realized in 1913 that he could not govern through progressives only, so after a brief flirtation with his past he learned by 1916 that he could not govern through conservatives only. While in those years the Republican leadership, with a suicidal fascination for the interests of business alone, opposed the Democratic program, Wilson within the Democracy effected a dynamic reconciliation of many interests, recruiting thereby a strong coalition composed of farmers, laborers, intellectuals, white collar people and a significant minority of businessmen who chose not to conform to the atrophied, timorous consensus of their calling. He could not, as it happened, for long restrain the centrifugal forces within this coalition, but at the height of his season he blazed the way that Franklin Roosevelt later followed. In the process he altered and enriched the original New Freedom and enlarged the base of the Democracy.

"Every man," Wilson once wrote, "who tries to guide the counsels of a great nation . . . should feel that his voice is lifted upon the chorus and that it is only the crown of the common theme." So it was with him. From the diversity represented by his counselors he gauged the common theme. He gave it at times a cadenced gospel. To its satisfaction he directed the legislative process. In particular he succeeded through the agency of his developing party in translating into policy the matured intentions of his environment. In situations where the party constituted a less effective agency, where the directive temper of society was less mature, he had more trouble. By the fall of 1916 his foreign policy had revealed this.

V

"The Force of Moral Principle"
1913–1917

IN ALL THE YEARS of his self-conscious preparation for high public office, Woodrow Wilson, as he admitted himself, gave little thought to the conduct of foreign affairs. The relative isolation of the United States
during the late nineteenth century permitted him, like
most of his countrymen, to indulge in a comfortable disinclination to examine either the bases or the processes of
foreign policy. He was therefore distracted, often de-
jected, by the succession of delicate and vexatious problems that increasingly captured the energies of his administration. The gravity of the responsibilities that befell
him would have troubled any feeling man. But Wilson was
especially disturbed because the attitudes of which he
fashioned foreign policy were so continually, so poign-
antly inappropriate to the emerging barbarity of the con-
temporaneous world.

"The force of America," Wilson asserted during one
crisis, "is the force of moral principle . . . there is nothing else that she loves, and . . . there is nothing else for
which she will contend." Moral principle, he believed,

precluded exploitative imperialism, which he took to be one source of modern wars. Partly on this account, moral principle entailed the duty to work for peace, both by example and, when necessary, through neutral mediation. American progressives by and large shared these assumptions. Accustomed as they were to attribute all evil at home to the greedy corruption of corporations, they assigned to those familiar devils, allegedly engaged in a ruthless rivalry for markets and profits, the full responsibility for militarism, colonialism and war.

Moreover, many Americans shared Wilson's conviction that Anglo-American constitutional arrangements, like much of the rest of Anglo-Saxon culture, had somehow a special moral as well as historical basis, that the United States had a predestined obligation to bring constitutionalism to the world, and that the people of semideveloped countries either would welcome this American export or should be taught to welcome it. Wilson therefore made an evangelical didacticism one popular foundation of his foreign policy. He proceeded also, again with much popular support, on the conviction that constitutionalism had an international equivalent in a body of law which, he presumed, defined and governed — or should be made to govern — the relations among nations. Moral principle held every nation not only itself to obey this law but also to insist upon obedience to it by others. A fervid legalism, then, a missionary constitutionalism tinged with racialism, a sentimental pacifism shaped Wilson's foreign policy.

Partly because he failed systematically to consult the expert intelligences in the executive departments and the foreign service, Wilson fell into traps formed by his own sentiments. Aware though he was of his own unfamiliarity with foreign policy, he selected as Secretary of State another amateur, Bryan, who harbored the very attitudes that at once inspired and handicapped his chief. These same ideas made Secretary of the Navy Josephus Daniels, a crony of Bryan, unsympathetic to the duties of his office, uninformed and uncommunicative about the large demands of military strategy. Furthermore, Bryan appointed "deserving Democrats" to diplomatic posts where other qualifications were needed, a practice the President permitted; and Wilson entrusted critical diplomatic missions to other innocents. Sure of the virtue of their intentions, supported by the naïveté alike of their staff and their constituency, President and Secretary of State let their untutored instincts obscure what informed analysis might have illuminated. The complex of their attitudes not only beclouded national interest but also conflicted on occasions of moment with Wilson's sincere abomination of imperialism and war.

So it happened that in the name of friendship Wilson ultimately took up a white man's burden scarcely distinguishable in form or in reward from that of less altruistic statesmen. Striving to set right the wrongs of imperialism he found on the nation's record, he withdrew American support from an international consortium formed during Taft's administration to finance a Chinese railroad. He also negotiated a treaty with Colombia providing both indemnity and apology for Theodore Roosevelt's unconscionable taking of Panama. But elsewhere in the Caribbean, though he intended to cultivate friendships, though he hoped to alleviate poverty and ignorance, he defeated his own purpose. Accepting his predecessors' practice of using American bankers to underwrite and supervise the finances of the perennially bankrupt republics there, Wilson not only perpetuated a kind of dollar diplomacy he would not countenance in China, but also unwittingly confined himself to the limitations of his unofficial banker-agents. Their counsel, ordinarily self-interested, ordinarily reaffirmed by Bryan's "deserving Democrats," provided an inadequate guide for cultivating friendship, especially since Wilson considered this objective "possible only when supported at every turn by the orderly processes of just government based upon law, not upon arbitrary or irregular force."

Badly advised, he let Bryan sustain unpopular, reactionary administrations in Nicaragua and Santo Domingo. After months of inept negotiation and indecision, he used American marines to establish protectorates in Santo Domingo and, against fierce resistance, in Haiti. The chaotic inability of those countries to govern themselves, the importance of stability in an area so strategically crucial as the Caribbean, made necessary Wilson's intercessions; but a more practiced diplomacy might have contained American problems before military intervention became a poor, last resort. There was, furthermore, no virtue in confusing the administrations Bryan sponsored or the marines created with just governments based on law. This delusion kept Wilson from appreciating the resentment of Latin Americans against any Yankee interference; it kept him also from seeing the potential dangers in his own unselfish intentions when conditions in a nation less backward than Haiti aroused his determination to make things just.

Such a nation was Mexico, where by 1913 revolution had entered a sanguinary stage. During the late nineteenth century, the large landholders, the army, the Catholic Church and foreign investors sustained in Mexico a government capable of suppressing the mass of the population

— landless, uneducated, exploited Indians and mestizos. In 1911 this government was overthrown. But efforts to remake Mexico engendered a resistance to which General Victoriano Huerta gave furtive direction. In February, 1913, Huerta accomplished a *coup d'état,* murdering his chief and re-establishing a government committed to the preservation of traditional privilege. At once the forces opposed to Huerta organized in northern Mexico the continuing revolution. These Constitutionalists selected as their leader Venustiano Carranza, who was to prove himself an adroit, implacable, and dedicated manager of traumatic change. In spite of the Constitutionalist movement, however, the major powers considered Huerta sufficiently in control to extend to him official recognition, and President Taft delayed only because he hoped first to extract Huerta's agreement to various American claims.

But Wilson set his face against Huerta. Unmoved by the demands of Americans with financial interests in Mexico, the President would not recognize a government of assassins. Unwilling therefore to name an ambassador, he sent instead a series of special agents, friends of his or Bryan's, who brought to their task liberal sentiments but no knowledge of Mexico. While their reports intensified both Wilson's laudable disgust with Huerta and his wise concern for social reform in Mexico, their insensitivity to local affairs encouraged his naïve belief that he could formulate and decree a solution to that country's problems. He never really learned that all factions in Mexico considered his repeated intrusions unwarranted invasions.

A first crisis arose in October, 1913, when Huerta, sustained by British oil interests, set himself up as military dictator, head of a government based beyond a doubt upon irregular and arbitrary force. Wilson now terminated his

announced policy of "watchful waiting." He would instead "require Huerta's retirement" by "such means as may
be necessary"; he would "teach the South American republics to elect good men!" To quiet Mexican fears, he declared publicly that the United States would never again
seek any land by conquest; he announced also his characteristic purpose to develop "constitutional liberty," to advance the world toward "those great heights where there
shines unobstructed the light of the justice of God."

To cut off Huerta's support, Wilson had to engineer a
reversal of British policy. To this end he promised to protect British property should a Constitutionalist victory
endanger it. He also pressed, as he might have in any case,
the repeal by Congress of a law exempting American
coastal shipping from tolls for the use of the Panama
Canal, a law the British considered a violation of an
American treaty guarantee. Gratified by these developments, forced by the imminence of war in Europe to
solicit Wilson's friendship, the British in March, 1914,
withdrew their recognition of Huerta.

Wilson by then had made the incredible proposal to
Carranza that the United States would join him in a war
against Huerta if Carranza would confine the revolution
to the orderly and the constitutional. A dedicated revo-
lutionary, adamantly opposed to American interference,
Carranza refused. Because he wanted American recognition, however, and needed arms which the American embargo denied him, he let his representative assure the
President that the Constitutionalists would respect the
rights of property. Wilson could then either do nothing
and let Huerta reign or take Carranza on his word and lift
the arms embargo. In February he chose the latter course.

But neither the neutrality of the British nor the armies

of the Constitutionalists unseated Huerta. Impatient to see the light of justice shine in Mexico, the President therefore made of a minor episode an excuse himself to intervene with force. On April 10 at Tampico an Huertista colonel arrested some American sailors who had come ashore. The colonel's commanding general immediately apologized to Admiral Henry T. Mayo, ranking American officer in the area. But Mayo, not satisfied with this, demanded a twenty-one-gun salute to the American flag, which the Mexicans refused. Electing to support Mayo, Wilson prepared plans to occupy Veracruz, Mexico's most important Caribbean port, and on April 20 asked Congress for authority to use military force "to obtain from General Huerta . . . the fullest recognition of the rights and dignity of the United States." If armed conflict were to result, Wilson told Congress, the United States would "be fighting only General Huerta and those who adhere to him . . . and our object would be only to restore to the people of the distracted republic the opportunity to set up again their . . . own government."

Armed conflict came the next day. To prevent a German merchant ship from landing arms for Huerta at Veracruz, Wilson without awaiting congressional action on his request ordered the navy to seize that city. Partly because Wilson did not explain the immediate reason for the bloodshed and the occupation that followed, he seemed to have acted only to force Huerta to salute. This was, regrettably, some part of his motive. Confused as he was by his own uninformed intentions, while he championed peace and justice in Mexico, he seemed, like the jingoes, ready "to blow up the whole place." Indeed, he set his military staffs to work on plans for all-out war.

Fortunately it did not come, for Wilson accepted the

mediation of Argentina, Brazil and Chile. He expected, however, to make mediation an instrument for arranging Mexican affairs. Insisting that no solution had "prospect of permanence" unless it removed Huerta, he also told the American negotiators that any settlement had to include "necessary agrarian and political reforms." But the agreement, pledging the United States to leave Veracruz without seeking any indemnity, contained no provision for removing Huerta, for reform, or for the salute Mayo had never received. It was not even signed by the Constitutionalists, who had become by June the dominant faction in Mexico. Through his negotiators, moreover, Carranza rejected out of hand American aid and American advice. Huerta, his fortunes spent, abdicated in July, but when Carranza marched into Mexico City in August, 1914, he owed fealty to no one.

Rebuffed by Carranza and still resolved to make of revolution a venture in polite reform, Wilson mixed further in Mexican affairs. One of Carranza's ablest lieutenants, Pancho Villa, was preparing to rebel against his chief. With the consummate skill of perfected rascality, Villa persuaded Wilson's gullible agents that he was a properly restrained and cooperative sort of revolutionist. When Villa's revolt began, Wilson therefore supported his corps of bandits. This was a calamity, for Carranza, giving masterful direction simultaneously to social revolution and civil war, held the allegiance of the Mexican people and during the summer of 1915 drove Villa and his dwindling band to guerilla retreats in their native north. Wilson's gamble only intensified Carranza's ire.

By this time the revolution had reached high fever. Violence accompanied reform as Constitutionalist leaders permitted, sometimes encouraged, the destruction of private property, much of it foreign-owned, and the barbaric treatment of the Roman Catholic clergy, so long identified with reaction. In the United States, especially among Catholics, interventionist sentiment grew, fanned by jingoes and Republican politicians. But Carranza's compelling victories made it obvious that the only means of disciplining him was general war. This Wilson could not afford. Increasingly engaged in troubles with Germany, at last sadly aware — as he admitted — that the violence of the revolution could not be talked away, Wilson in October, 1915, accepted Carranza on Carranza's terms and recognized the *de facto* existence of the Constitutionalist regime.

Pancho Villa then showed his real self to Wilson. Determined to embarrass Carranza by provoking the United States, Villa in January, 1916, murdered a group of Americans he had taken from a train in Mexico, and in March, in a raid on Columbia, New Mexico, killed nineteen more. The Republican and Catholic press spurred American demands for massive retribution. But Wilson, convinced though he was that Carranza either could not or would not discipline Villa, retaliated on a limited scale only. He ordered an expedition to cross the border and punish Villa but to avoid engaging any Constitutionalists.

The futile chase of Villa excited Mexican opinion. Carranza in April demanded that the Americans withdraw. After Wilson refused, while negotiations to arrange a withdrawal on mutually satisfactory terms faltered, Villa boldly raided Texas, Wilson called up the national guard for duty on the border, and the army prepared for a full-scale invasion of Mexico. Twice American and Carranzista soldiers skirmished, the second episode almost precipitating war. But Carranza's preoccupation with domestic troubles, Wilson's need to be unfettered in his dealings with the belligerent powers in Europe, and the genuine desire of both men for peace prompted them in July to agree to appoint a joint commission to resolve their differences. Although Carranza in December rejected the joint commission's protocol, the danger of war had by then been averted. Unwilling to occupy northern Mexico, especially with war near in Europe, Wilson in January, 1917, ordered the troops to withdraw and in March extended to the Constitutionalists *de jure* recognition.

For four years Carranza had held to the terms he identified perceptively with his own and Mexico's best interests, gaining in the end the freedom from interference upon which he had continually insisted. Wilson, on the other hand, had failed to capture Villa just as he had failed to get Huerta to salute. Probably he hastened the fall of Huerta, but Constitutionalist resistance would doubtless have accomplished this in any case, especially after England became involved in the First World War. To Wilson's credit, he had seen the need for social reform; he had avoided the general war with Mexico that many American investors, Catholics, and professional patriots coveted. But his support of Villa served neither reform nor order nor peace, and his armed reprisals, violations of Mexican sovereignty, brought the two countries perilously close to unnecessary war.

The United States, Wilson had appreciated, could ill afford to try to protect American property or the Catholic Church in the imbroglio of revolution, but it could afford no better by intrigue or force to try to teach its neighbors to elect good men. That tendentious effort generated the smug bombast that can breed vainglorious war. This, to be sure, was precisely what Wilson deplored. For himself and for his country, his muddled purpose had worked ironic mischief.

The stakes were vastly higher during the long uncertainty of American policy that began in August, 1914, with the outbreak of hostilities in Europe. Then, after more than a decade of tension and sporadic crises, the two great alliances — Great Britain, France and Russia; Germany, Austria-Hungary and Turkey — surrendered themselves and the whole world to the devastating test of modern war. But for meeting the problems of World War I, Wilson and Bryan, like most Americans, were totally unprepared. From the first, the President's definitions of neutrality revealed the innocence of his assumptions.

He had faith, to begin with, that the United States successfully could "speak the counsels of peace and accommodation," play "a part of impartial mediation." He had earlier supported Bryan's negotiation of thirty "cooling off" treaties that provided for the submission to an international commission of disputes diplomacy failed to settle. Signatories agreed to abjure hostilities during the year these commissions had to investigate and report. "Whenever any trouble arises," Wilson had remarked of these treaties, "the light shall shine on it for a year before anything is done; and my prediction is that after the light has shone on it . . . it will not be necessary to do anything. . . . Moral light . . . is the most wholesome and rectifying . . . thing in the world."

Although Germany had declined to sign a conciliation treaty, although Austria had refused to submit to arbitration the Serbian question that precipitated general war in Europe, Wilson nourished the hope that through him the light would shine. He persisted even though his efforts at mediation elicited from neither side any terms but those tantamount to victory. His hope, moreover, induced him to underestimate the nationalistic tensions, the suspicions, the considerations of power politics that moved the chancelleries of Europe, the intense, pervasive force of unreasoning emotions that belligerency spawned.

Wilson also urged his country to "be neutral in fact as well as in name . . . impartial in thought as well as in action." Believing, as did many progressives, that the war had nothing to do with the United States, he avoided for almost three years any assessment of its causes. His appeal for impartiality confirmed, superficially at least, the theory that selfish, commercial, imperialistic rivalries in a corrupt Europe brought about a war which it was the duty of the United States to avoid, a war that would otherwise divert men of good hope from refurbishing democracy at home. But nothing could prevent the obvious partiality that the President and most of his countrymen immediately and increasingly displayed. Americans of various national origins identified themselves with the loyalties of their forebears; so the German-Americans and Irish-Americans in particular gave emotional support to the Central Powers; the English-, Scotch-, Welsh- and French-Americans in particular favored the western Allies. The latter were the larger group. The sameness of British and American speech and institutions, furthermore, fostered a sympathy for England that Wilson could not help but share. He had always believed, after all, that American history was simply an extension of British experience.

Partiality among Americans was accentuated by British stories of atrocities allegedly committed by German soldiers, by German accounts of mass starvation allegedly caused by the British blockade. But the hyperbole of propaganda and, perhaps, even the prejudices of vicarious nationalism had less effect on American opinion than did the course of the war itself. Germany's invasion of Belgium, violating the treaty pledging the German Empire to respect Belgian neutrality, made her seem to be, as she was, a deliberate aggressor, an impression reinforced by subsequent events and revelations. (Indeed, however general the guilt for the underlying causes of the war may have been, the German general staff had made and timed its plans so as to earn an accolade for perfidy it was in time to earn again.)

All this made neutrality of thought impossible. Wilson's continuing assumption that it existed impeded the development of American policy, as did his uncritical assumption that it should have existed, for he left uninvestigated the question of the strategic importance to the United States of aggression in western Europe. He was criticized for failing to protest Germany's invasion of Belgium on legal and moral grounds; he was much more remiss for neglecting to reckon whether this invasion endangered the balance of power.

The President simply did not think in terms of national security. This was true also in the Orient, where the tradition of American intervention existed, fortified by treaties negotiated during previous administrations. When Japan, capitalizing on Europe's troubles, in 1915 demanded from China political and economic concessions making China for all intents and purposes a protectorate, Bryan with Wilson's support warned that the United States would not recognize any agreement impairing American treaty rights or China's political or territorial integrity. Bryan's note sustained the principles of the Open Door policy and asserted his doctrine that denied recognition to the conquests of aggressors. Neither he nor Wilson, however, calculated whether the interests of the United States were larger in the Orient, about which they spoke out, than in Europe, about which they said nothing. Although the situations in both continents needed to be controlled, in dealing with them Wilson was the passive captive of traditions he consecrated.

This moral cast of Wilson's mind kept him from examining the full implications of neutrality. He permitted mistaken sentiments to flourish, as time went by to condition and confuse responses to the doctrines about neutral rights in which, with small reference to national needs, he and most of his countrymen let themselves believe.

Resolved from the time the war began to uphold neutral rights to trade and the use of the ocean — traditional American concerns — Wilson had to strike discriminatory postures. Since England would not accept the definitions of neutral rights in the Declaration of London, which she had never signed, Wilson in September, 1914, accepted as his substitute standard "the existing rules of international law and the treaties of the United States." But these, at best unsure, had little relevance to conditions of modern total war, especially to the then unprecedented tactics of the submarine, Germany's indispensable naval weapon. With both England and Germany, therefore, but particularly with the latter, large troubles soon arose over Wilson's legalistic interpretations of American neutral rights.

The British, controlling the seas, were determined that the Allies alone should profit from American shipments of munitions and other materials essential for their successful prosecution of the war. Establishing a tight blockade of Germany, they limited narrowly the kinds of goods American or other neutral ships could carry to neutral ports from which transshipments could reach Germany, diverted suspect shipping to British ports, confiscated many cargoes, let others spoil, interfered with American mails to intercept information pertinent to the military or economic aspects of the war, ultimately forbade British subjects to do any business with a large number of American firms accused of violating British rules.

Wilson protested repeatedly and vigorously against these and other practices, some of which indisputably infringed upon traditional neutral rights. To a nation engaged in total war his protests seemed peevishly legalistic. But the British, recognizing their dependence upon American supplies, executed skillfully the central policy of their diplomacy, "to secure the maximum of blockade that could be enforced without a rupture with the United States."

The success of this policy owed much to the fellowship Americans felt for the Allies and to the continual cooperation with the British foreign office of the fervently pro-British United States ambassador, but the irritable accord preserved between the English-speaking nations owed perhaps as much to the growing economic stake of the United States in war production, and more to an increasing American animosity toward Germany. Allied demand for war materials not only stimulated American heavy industry but also provided a growing market for American agriculture, which would have faced distress had trade been terminated. With a wise solicitude, prompted by Wilson's pleas, for the continuing prosperity of American cotton farmers, the British even provided funds to stabilize the price of cotton at a level acceptable to the Democratic South.

No rule for neutral duties prevented Americans from selling the Allies the material for their arsenals. Indeed, had Wilson by redefining neutral duties refused to permit this trade, he would in effect have made himself a partner of Germany and her associates on the continent. Modern war simply made true neutrality a chimera. Where there were rules about contraband of war governing the kinds of things that could be carried on American rather than on Allied bottoms, Wilson tried to observe them. But often he had only his scruples by which to steer. These let Bryan briefly hold that loans by American bankers to finance Allied purchases in the United States violated "the true spirit of neutrality." Money, Bryan had argued, was the worst contraband of all. Nevertheless, early in 1915, when the Allies needed aid, Bryan with Wilson's blessing partially reversed himself, and by the end of that year the State Department had endorsed the enormous loans arranged by American bankers without which France and England simply could not have continued to buy. Thereafter, to almost every segment of the American economy, as informed Americans came gradually to realize, a break with England or a German triumph would have brought hardship and perhaps disaster.

The Germans, unable to transport supplies through the British blockade, not only complained about the American sales of articles of war and British interpretations of maritime rules, but also, more effectively, sent into the Atlantic, especially into the waters around the British Isles, a fleet of submarines to destroy the supplies France and England needed. The submarine of World War I, however, like its deadlier descendants, could not operate in accordance with the rules for the conduct of commerce destroyers in earlier, more genteel wars. Submarine tactics precluded any warning to a prospective target or removal of its crew and passengers before a sinking; the small size and vulnerability of submarines prevented the rescue of survivors. Yet Wilson insisted, as Americans by and large believed he should, that tenuous interpretations of traditional international law confine the submarines.

The submarine issue arose in February, 1915, when Germany, proclaiming a war zone around the British Isles, warned that enemy ships would be sunk on sight and neutral ships would be in danger because of British misuse of neutral flags. Wilson admonished the British not to fly the Stars and Stripes, a ruse that was nonetheless never abandoned. To Germany, however, he sent a sharper, more portentous note, describing the sinking of merchantmen without visit and search as "a wanton act" and declaring that the destruction of American ships or American lives on belligerent ships would be regarded as "a flagrant violation of neutral rights," offensive if not hostile to the United States, for which he would hold the German government to a "strict accountability." This posture reflected the general American unawareness of the inherent, unrestrainable barbarity of modern weapons. It also prevented the genuine neutrality that Wilson professedly cultivated, for the Germans could not afford by abandoning the submarine to clear the highway for the Allies' supplies. The use of the submarine, moreover, was bound to give rise to incidents that would test Wilson's definition of strict accountability and force him ultimately, for the defense of that formulation, to forsake with reluctance his devout wish for peace.

Incidents came quickly: an American lost aboard a British ship in April, 1915; an American ship torpedoed the first of May; six days later the sinking of the British passenger liner *Lusitania,* with the attendant death of hundreds of men, women and children, many of them Americans. This shocked the entire country. A minority of Americans, already committed to the Allied cause, already angered by a German advertisement that had warned Americans not to sail on the *Lusitania,* now wanted to break relations with Germany, a nation in their view guilty, as Theodore Roosevelt put it, of "piracy" and "murder." Most men of this mind hoped soon to see the United States at war. German- and Irish-Americans and others sympathetic to Germany, those also who wished a plague on every warring house, were prepared to arbitrate the issue, if necessary to prohibit travel on belligerent ships, in any event to avoid a break with Germany. Most Americans, falling between these polar groups, were enraged by the sinking, for which they wanted some redress, but were also anxious to avoid hostility or even to abandon official neutrality. Like Wilson, they hoped the problem could be negotiated away.

Indeed, the President, sure of the righteousness of his position and the persuasiveness of his prose, believed he could talk Germany into relinquishing her weapon. "There is such a thing as a man being too proud to fight," he told one audience. "There is such a thing as a nation being so right that it does not need to convince others by force that it is right." Beginning negotiations in this spirit, Wilson had no ear for the German arguments excusing the sinking on the grounds that the *Lusitania* carried ammunition as well as passengers (as she had), and the British blockade starved German women and children (as it did not). Such considerations, he replied, were secondary, for the United States was contending for "something much greater than mere rights of property," for "nothing less high and sacred than the rights of humanity." "Illegal and inhuman acts," he asserted, were "manifestly indefensible," especially when they deprived neutrals of their "acknowledged rights," particularly "the right to life itself." The United States would therefore under no conditions consent "to abate any essential or fundamental right of its people." Wilson requested not just apology and reparation; recognizing explicitly that submarines could not be used without inevitable violations of "many sacred principles of justice and humanity," he demanded in effect that they be not used at all.

Wilson's reliance alone upon an exchange of notes with Germany struck Theodore Roosevelt and like-minded militants as proof the President was "yellow," but the tone of the notes seemed to Bryan unduly and dangerously harsh. The Secretary of State, speaking the hopes of the agrarian progressives who had for so long seen life through lenses just like his own, had urged Wilson both to protest to England because the *Lusitania* carried ammunition and to indicate to Germany that the question could be settled according to the principles of the "cooling off" treaties. At first amenable to the latter suggestion, Wilson abandoned it after other counselors convinced him that it would damage his case against Germany and vitiate his leadership at home. Increasingly troubled after Wilson's change of mind, unable to see in transatlantic travel any sacred right, sadly aware that from the high plateau of morality his chief had ascended there might be no descent except into the war he dreaded, Bryan resigned. To his place Wilson appointed the Counselor of the Department of State, Robert Lansing, an urbane New York lawyer. "Capable, industrious, meticulous, metallic and mousy," the new Secretary was also demonstrably and contentedly proficient in clothing Wilson's moral insights in legal phraseology and in reflecting, as did the President, the drifting purpose of the majority of Americans.

This purpose prevailed when Germany in February, 1916, met Wilson halfway. The Imperial Government would not admit the illegality of the *Lusitania* or any other sinking, but it expressed regret over the loss of American lives, for which it offered an indemnity. In a statement accompanying this offer, the German chancellor explained to the American people that he could do no more, for he could not permit the submarine to be neutralized. Wilson, the Democratic party leaders, and by and large the American people accepted with relief the German apology and explanation. The United States, as Lansing put it, desired only honorable friendship.

But new difficulties kept this goal at a distracting remove. Captured by the prevalent American assumption that war had rules, Wilson and Lansing had tried to persuade the western powers to stop arming merchantmen. Armed merchants, they pointed out, gave submarines no choice in tactics; if the ships were not armed, Germany might agree to warn all vessels before sinking them. The Germans were naturally charmed by this negotiation, for their purpose was not to kill sailors but to sink cargoes and bottoms. They apparently took Lansing in, for when the British of course refused to make sitting ducks of their merchant fleet, Lansing suggested to the Germans that they declare unrestricted submarine warfare against armed ships. This the Germans did with unconcealed delight. The British, however, greeted the announcement not by capitulating, as Wilson and Lansing had more or less expected, but with a customary stiff-upper resistance. Lansing then doubled back. If the Allies would not disarm merchantmen, he declared, the United States would have to adhere to the old rules of war. According to these as Wilson had interpreted them, a submarine sinking a ship, especially one carrying Americans, without first giving warning, violated sacred human principles.

With the Germans standing by their torpedoes, the British by their guns, and Wilson by strict accountability, the critics of the President had cause for their doubts. By irritating and embarrassing the British, he had alienated further those who favored the Allies. On this front the Roosevelt Republicans prepared to pitch a part of the impending presidential campaign. He had also drawn the Germans into taking a position he would not now condone, thereby inviting a new *Lusitania* case and possibly a war. To this prospect agrarian progressives and their spokesmen at once responded. There was, they believed, a "sort of moral treason" in letting American citizens create crises by risking their lives on belligerent ships. Only such artificial issues, they were sure, made the war any concern of the United States. Resolutions they drafted to forbid the controversial travel won support in both houses of Congress among influential Democrats, some representing districts with large German-American populations, some simply imbued with views like Bryan's.

Wilson had brought himself to this serious pass. Without questioning the policies that had failed him at home and abroad, he fought himself out of it. "Once accept a single abatement of right," he told the rebellious Democrats, "and many other humiliations would follow, and the whole fine fabric of international law might crumble under our hands." "The honor and self-respect of the nation" were involved. "We covet peace," he explained, "and shall preserve it at any cost but the loss of honor."

Even for Southern Democrats, this talk of law and honor was probably less convincing than the presence in the lobbies of the Postmaster General, conservator of party discipline. The obvious and clumsy efforts of the German-American Alliance in opposition to the President also helped his case. When he thought he had the upper hand, he demanded a speedy vote, warning that reports of divided counsels in Washington were doing "the greatest harm" in foreign capitals. Joined, indeed led, by Eastern Republicans, enough Democrats voted Wilson's way to table the contentious resolutions.

A more crucial test of Wilson's policy came within the month when on March 24, 1916, a submarine without warning torpedoed the French channel steamer *Sussex*. Taking the advice of House and Lansing, after some temporizing hesitation Wilson at last prepared an ultimatum. As he told Congress on April 19, it had "become painfully evident that the position which this Government took at the very outset is inevitable, namely, that the use of submarines . . . is of necessity . . . incompatible with the principles of humanity, the long established and incontrovertible rights of neutrals, and the sacred immunities of noncombatants."

"Unless the Imperial Government should now immediately declare and effect an abandonment of its present method of submarine warfare against passenger and freight-carrying vessels," Lansing instructed Berlin, the United States would "have no choice but to sever diplomatic relations."

Neither the legal nor the moral argument swayed the Germans. For a season, however, the kaiser's council was dominated by those like his chancellor who calculated that continued American neutrality would be of greater use to

Germany than would unrestricted submarine warfare. On May 4 Germany therefore agreed that submarines would observe the rules of visit and search. But the German note went on with overbearing condescension to threaten to reverse this decision unless the United States compelled the British to obey international law. Lansing, sensing duplicity in this reservation, was prepared, as was a growing but still minority opinion, to reject the German reply. Wilson, however, ignoring the reservation and reaffirming strict accountability, accepted the slender concession Germany had made.

Once again most Americans were relieved; some, ebullient. To them the President seemed to have mastered the torpedo with his pen. But this was an illusion, for the *Sussex* pledge committed Germany only to a conditional self-restraint subject to removal at any time her leaders recalculated their advantage. Should the fortunes of war change, should the military and naval leaders of Germany gain the command of government, the submarines would resume their predatory manner. Wilson, though he interpreted it otherwise, had elicited no pledge at all.

He had also made the submarine issue brittle. Identifying it with the sacred, the moral, the honorable, the humane, he not only registered his own inflexibility but also left his country defending ideological fortresses it could not, without a prodigious loss of prestige, desert. A reversal of German policy would leave the United States no recourse but severance of relations which, given the situation, could only be a way-station toward war.

For this eventuality, furthermore, Wilson had prepared neither his mind nor his people's. The source of war in Europe, the potential source then and afterwards of possible war for the United States, lay in situations utterly

unrelated to rules for sinking merchantmen. The world
had become too small, the affairs of nations too intercon-
nected, to permit any country an immunity from war. It
was not only a question of national security. Even in terms
of morality, Wilson neglected to ask himself whether the
position of neutrality was really tolerable. As he knew,
large elements of force cannot withdraw from civil society
without inviting anarchy. But he did not question
whether, in international society, the United States could
play the part of a Sweden or a Switzerland without abandoning the moral responsibility of great power.

Very few Americans thought about this. On one side
of Wilson were the immovable noninterventionists, like
Bryan, who still believed that a policy of nonintercourse
could isolate the United States from what they took to be
an irrelevant episode, the handiwork of malignant con-
spirators. Not even two hot wars and one cold one have
completely dispelled their fallacy. On the other side of
Wilson were interventionists like Roosevelt, some of them
more conscious than was the President of the American
stake in the course of European affairs. Many of them,
however, were motivated either by an irrational belief in
the automatic justice of any British cause — a belief that
tempted but did not envelop the President — or by an
equally irrational assumption that some abstract good inhered in using or in rattling sabers, an adolescent reverie
the President scorned.

Most Americans stood on a middle ground with Wilson
and his admirers. They were men of great good will, not
foolish, but deplorably unschooled. They had almost no
experience from which to draw their judgments. National
policy for decades past had traditionally been neutral, had
traditionally defended neutral rights. The sinking of mer-

chantmen by submarines, futhermore, however much a part of war, was a terrible thing. Established habits of mind, natural instincts of horror, led President and people to pursue or approve policies on faith alone.

Precisely because the directive temper of society was unsure, the burden of leadership lay heavily on Wilson. He always did his honest best. Had he been able to understand and explain the situation more perceptively than he did, perhaps only a minority could have shed enough of their misapprehensions to understand him. As it was, not even a minority had that chance. Wilson not only lost himself in a tangential issue but also lost it in distorting sentiments. His neutrality policies, like his Mexican policies, sowed chauvinistic seeds. Ringing every change on morality and honor, he fed the self-righteous, martial spirit that, to his horror, Theodore Roosevelt hoped to make the common creed. Perhaps more damaging still, because no one talked sense to the American people, they remained confused about the war and consequently, in a gray afterlook, subject to hurt feelings and disillusionment.

Yet the *Sussex* pledge, coming as it did in May of an election year, gave a timely boost to Wilson's canvass. His apparent success, heartening to all Democrats, especially pleased progressives, who fancied war now thrust away. German-Americans, tense in their own ambivalence, sensitive to the suspicions of their neighbors, welcomed the respite the pledge afforded. With the Irish-Americans (whose animosity toward England had been exacerbated by the suppression of the Easter Rebellion, Ireland's bid with German aid for independence), they welcomed also the opportunity Wilson now found to protest anew several British practices. The President had long since alienated the extremists in both hyphenate groups, but the *Sussex* pledge preserved the loyalty of those moderates who had Democratic habits.

Followed as it was in June by the settlement in Mexico, the *Sussex* affair let Wilson appear the champion of righteousness and honor, peacefully triumphant through the "force of moral principle." As much as his achievements in domestic reform, as much as his deference to progressivism, perhaps more, this was to make him President again. After all, like Wilson, most Americans preferred their issues moral, their honor pure, their peace preserved. He sensed again the common theme. War and revolution, twin perils of the twentieth century, pain and puzzle any man. Along paths he would like to have avoided, Wilson had come by 1916 to the crossroads — not his alone, but his world's.

V I

The Fearful Things

1913–1917

AGAINST WHAT SEEMED at times to be overwhelming evidence, Woodrow Wilson sustained articles of faith common for several generations to the comfortable and polite in the United States and Europe. There was, he believed, an order in human affairs determined by God and perceivable by men. Though man was sinful and God scrupulously just, man had — he thought — a transcendent capacity to discover the rational arrangements within which his kind could wend in antiseptic harmony their several ways. This magic casement opened on a fairyland from which the perilous seas were charmed away. But like any fairyland, it needed protection from reality, from exposure to the violence and prejudice and lust that lay within the environment it was presumed to replace.

Not war alone, but the impact of a multitude of personal and social problems in Wilson's time called to question his optimistic rationalism and the doctrines he derived from it. Yet consistently he maintained positions that did not satisfy the data of his senses. This was not a matter of dishonesty. He had never much relied on data. But what was more important, he fixed his own security in the doctrines he promulgated. He could not afford to modify these doctrines for fear of losing hold of his personality. He had to live in a world made up in part of his illusions. In the case of so able a man as Wilson, this led to tragedy. As he met the needs of his own personality, it also led to statements rooted in illusion, but, for that very reason, statements that transcended the apparent limits of reality, statements that composed man's most precious dreams and grandest faiths.

Wilson's private model for political behavior suffered first of all from his lack of joy, his protective diffidence that built a wall between him and other men. He never knew the kind of fellowship that eased the burden of both Roosevelts' days; he never had their saving sense of humor. Forms of address reflected the President's distance. He was "Woodrow" to no political associate; not one of them did he call by his given name. Beyond the borders of the parlor this stiffness remained. Without a sense of playfulness in men, the President denied a place to playfulness in politics, insulated himself from the lessons taught by fun, choked off that flood of fondness Americans display for leaders who evoke it.

He could never understand how large a part of politics is masculine good-fellowship whose sinews bind men unmoved by any other cause. The glad, spontaneous hand made him uncomfortable. Professional politicians, uncomfortable in turn, distressed by what they took to be the President's ingratitude to his sometime associates, increasingly distrusted him. One of them, one also of Wilson's most adulating admirers, ruefully admitted when Theodore Roosevelt died in 1919 that Americans had lost the President they loved.

Yet Wilson did not live in frigid isolation, for Ellen

Wilson gave him strength and love. Her gentleness mellowed even his austerity; her thoughtfulness made him considerate beyond his inclinations. She was a great lady. For any man such a wife would have been important; for Wilson she was indispensable. Her untimely death in 1914 *Ellen* left him in a frosty loneliness no human being pierced for many months, left him crippled emotionally just when events in Europe and in Mexico called upon his reserves of nerve and understanding as nothing ever had before. Then for a time his isolation was practically complete. His daughters, the doting lady cousins who enlarged his entourage, his doctor and his secretary were at once disturbed and helpless.

The intolerable ended when his physician introduced him to a handsome widow, Edith Bolling Galt, a strong, intelligent, patrician, ambitious woman. She did the most important thing that could be done for Wilson: she made him smile again. After a swift romance they married in December, 1915. The sniffing of Edwardian noses at what Edwardian manners took to be his haste was insignificant; the intrusion of Mrs. Galt's unsettling personality was not. The second Mrs. Wilson, in contrast to the first, resented those who shared her husband's confidences, personal or political. Unlike the first, she could not find dignity or wisdom in men unblessed with pedigree. She was in many trying hours a loving and a loyal wife, but she also, sometimes inadvertently, in many trying ways set out to exclude from Wilson's life the very associations that tended most effectively to moderate his starkness.

She found an ally in Colonel House. Like the President's lady cousins, House had become a part of Wilson's home while Ellen Wilson still presided there. Apperceptive of his place, he made it a rule, in treating with Wilson, to listen more than he spoke, to concur when he could with enthusiasm, never openly to disagree. His amiable passivity, his whispered confidences, the transparent codes that made his simplest messages seem conspiratorial, revealed a sly effeminacy that won for him associate membership in the sorority at the White House. The colonel, furthermore, had a large talent for small intrigue, indeed a kind of fascination with it. In the shifting jealousies and ambitions of those around the President he found a splendid laboratory, especially attractive because Wilson seemed intent upon ignoring the rivalries for his favor. In the palace of his dreams there had, apparently, been no jostling near the throne. Now it began.

This was not entirely House's doing. He simply exploited the personal, attitudinal and sectional frictions that beset all administrations. A network of associates, grateful for his favors, from their sensitive positions kept him informed. This group included, among others, Postmaster General Burleson and Attorney General Thomas Gregory, Assistant Secretary of State Frank Polk, Vance McCormick, Robert C. Woolley and Daniel C. Roper — the last three, thanks to House's influence, by 1916 the staffs and stays of the Democratic National Committee. Intermittently in but never of the group were Dr. Cary Grayson, the President's personal physician, and Secretary of the Treasury McAdoo, who even before he married Wilson's daughter considered himself heir apparent to the Presidency. Drawn to these and others like them, though one orbit further from the sun of House's charm, were such as John W. Davis, the Solicitor General, and young Franklin D. Roosevelt, then Assistant Secretary of the Navy.

These were, for the most part, talented, progressive and impatient men. Between them and the reforms they wanted for the country, between them and the careers they wanted for themselves, there lay the power and the inertia of the big Democratic machines. To the spokesmen of these organizations in Washington, House's young hounds gave chase, openly until divisive repercussions in New York State forced Wilson in 1914 to call them off, thereafter quietly but no less — or more — effectively. They succeeded by 1916 in reducing to an unprecedented (but transitory) minimum the influence within the party of America's Tammany Halls. This in itself helped in that year to win the progressive vote, so important in the Middle West and West. It also cost the party the dedication of its organizations in the East, thereby making that area then and later vulnerable to Republican incursions.

There were other, less obvious losses. Veterans of Democratic machine politics understood from first-hand experience a good deal about the needs of the urban unlettered that neither the agrarian liberal nor the well-born progressive could readily learn. To the extent that House and his friends gained dominance among the Wilsonians, the President tended to lose touch with those counselors who alone brought to the White House the Democracy of the city wards. Such men were not often proponents of tariff or trust or banking reforms. Frequently they were obsessed with, inevitably they were involved in, the small politics of local patronage. But ordinarily they also had a special sensibility for the dignity of the meanest among the working force, the Negro wandered North, the immigrant so recently a peasant, their children and their urban neighbors. Precisely because Wilson lacked that sensibility, he needed help from the kind of associates House's maneuverings endangered.

The distinctive democracy of such men, furthermore,

provided an indispensable counterweight to certain lamentable proclivities of progressivism. As it developed under Wilson and especially under House, progressive leadership fell largely to two groups. One, prominent also among Republican liberals, consisted of Northern business and professional men, dedicated, to be sure, to eliminating iniquity and corruption, but often almost hostile to the way of life of the laboring force, a way of life they attributed with hasty imperception primarily to blood and birth. The second group sprang from the South. Provincial where the others were stuffy, these aggressive critics of the economic order were also usually skittish defenders of a theory of race that sanctioned discrimination against the Negro in the South, a theory applied elsewhere against the yellow man or the brown man or against other intruders in the American dust whose skin was swarthy or whose accent strange. Those who worked for the city boss, by contrast, had to know and help these people. Indeed, these people or their children had in many places become the bosses or the bosses' heirs. In so far as House and Mrs. Galt kept Wilson from them, they deprived the President of antibiotics his Southernism needed.

Racial and religious prejudice, by no means peculiar to the South, developed broad currency as Southerners gained ascendancy within the federal government. Against this Wilson provided only an intermittent and uncertain leadership, perhaps because he could not conclusively overcome the heritage of his youth, perhaps because, as he contended, he had on occasion to submit to the wishes of the Southern congressmen. In any case he permitted several of his cabinet to segregate, for the first time since the Civil War, whites and Negroes within executive departments. Throughout the South the discharge or demotion of Negro federal employees attended the New Freedom. In response to liberal protests this in time was checked, but Wilson never openly took issue with the proponents of Jim Crow. So also in the West: while the California legislature worked out a bill insulting to the Japanese, a bill both unjust to Japanese-Americans and provocative of international tension, Wilson from first to last recommended only that statutory discrimination be phrased as inoffensively as possible.

Tolerant of discrimination based on pigmentation, Wilson, like many other Southerners, was also tolerant of discrimination based on sex. The woman's suffrage movement made its slowest progress in the South, where, among other attitudes, the sentimental vision of Lady Guinevere persuaded self-conscious Lancelots that the right to vote was male as well as white. Obviously fonder of women at the hearth than at the hustings, Wilson shielded his distaste for suffragettes by explaining that theirs was a problem to be solved not by the federal government but by the states. Southerners had said the same of slavery.

As with race and sex, so with religion. The bigoted, especially in the rural South, lived by regressive standards. There, transferring stereotypes of fear and hate from the Negro to the Jew and the Catholic, the politically irresponsible discovered new reservoirs of demagoguery. This kind of irrationality Wilson did resist. Indeed, defying it, in 1916 he appointed Brandeis, a Jew, to the Supreme Court; in 1913 he had made Tumulty, a Catholic, his personal secretary. But Catholic opposition to the President's Mexican policies and Irish-American hostility to his neutrality policies, intensifying anti-Catholicism as they were bound to, persuaded those who were susceptible to such persuasion that in no place of public trust would Americans condone a Catholic. So insinuated Mrs. Galt and Colonel House, both anxious on several counts to see Tumulty removed. Their tactic almost succeeded, for Wilson by 1916 was ready for a time to let himself be moved by the prejudice of others. This was uncomfortably akin to prejudice itself.

Stimulated by world conditions, exploited by divers groups, permeating gradually many quarters of American society, prejudice underlay an increasing sentiment for the restriction, even the exclusion, of immigration. Confused by a racialist sociology and Malthusian economics, labor leaders contended that mass immigration from southern and eastern Europe depressed American wages. Similarly confused, many progressives also found it easier to blame the immigrant for the slums than to rectify the conditions that made the slums the prisons of the immigrants. And in the rural South and West the xenophobia characteristic of populism persisted. These attitudes found expression in a bill which Congress passed in 1915 providing for a literacy test, a device intended to exclude the Italians and Greeks and Poles and others the restrictionists considered undesirable. So in some respects did Wilson, but as he had warned he would, he vetoed the measure. What bothered him particularly, he observed, was not the abridgment of the traditional right of asylum, not the confusion of capacity with literacy, but the lack of "conscious and universal assent" by the American people to the bill. "I have no pride of opinion in this question," he concluded, "I only want instruction." This kind of veto, leaving the door to further agitation open, did not seriously offend his Southern friends, especially since he took care to explain privately that his explicit promises in 1912 to groups of foreign extraction committed him to his decision. Within the President's heart there continued, clearly, a struggle between attitudes that had long shaped his thinking and those that politics demanded.

Not at home, nor among friends, nor in politics could Wilson factor out of his life the sentiments and compulsions that prevented him and his fellows from finding by some sure, rational process neat formulations for personal or social behavior. Worse still, the hope for so factoring diminished constantly. War not only brutalized Europe. It revealed to all Western men the awful power of organized passion, the naked vulnerability of intelligence and decency and orderliness. In this continent as well as that, the timid sought some impassioned symbol of their own. Inexorably aware as they were of the strains on their own loyalties, of the pluralistic nature of their culture, many Americans genuinely felt the need for some common super-loyalty; others saw advantages for themselves in such a thing. And feelings rose, here over labor conflicts, there about woman suffrage, elsewhere about Catholics or Germans, everywhere tending to merge into stereotypes that made optimism and rationalism alike remote. Those who most avidly supported the Allies most fervently demanded, by and large, a new "Americanism" unconditioned by any prior or peripheral loyalties to forebears, faith or friends. This standard also served those businessmen who had long considered any union foreign; it served, too, those who distrusted Negroes or Japanese, Catholics or Jews, gypsies or vegetarians. When next the literacy test became an issue, in 1917, Congress quickly overrode the President's veto. There remained by then small welcome for the strange.

Crown of the common theme, Wilson neither nurtured this oppressive spirit of conformity, as Roosevelt did, nor damped it, as Lincoln might have. Rather, he was part of it, carried along in spite of himself, quite unintentionally. Though inadvertently, the direction of his foreign policies bred chauvinism. However conditioned by politics, the directions of his thinking remained, as always, committed to interpreting America essentially as England's seedling. His culture, after all, was never pluralistic. Though he resisted prejudice, though he detested demagoguery, though he valued the tradition of dissent, he became sufficiently sensitive to "Americanism" to adopt a version of it as his own. His modifications were characteristic. In several public speeches he made "Americanism" a synonym for the self-conscious, idealized moralism of his foreign policy. Calling attention to the sabotage that interfered with the production of munitions for the Allies, late in 1915 he attributed this by implication to that extremist fringe of Irish- and German-Americans who most vociferously opposed his doctrines of neutrality. Condemning them, calling upon his countrymen for unmitigated dedication to what he considered national honor, he planned to make this Wilsonized "Americanism," strain that it was of a common species, the keynote of his campaign for re-election.

Wilson's appropriation of "Americanism" accompanied his belated recognition of the importance of preparedness, another issue raised by his opponents on the right. In spite of war, Wilson long persisted in the habit of optimistic mind that denied the existence of force as a factor in human affairs, that considered arms the dangerous and unnecessary tools of evil or of foolish men. Law and reason, in his model, governed the affairs of nations. Undeterred by the facts of aggression and bloodshed in Europe, he announced in December, 1914, his continuing opposition to both a large standing army and military training, his devotion to the traditional American dependence — born of eighteenth-century conditions — on a tiny army of professionals supplemented by a small militia, the National Guard, composed of part-time citizen-soldiers recruited on a voluntary basis and controlled by the states. Even the further development of the navy, a slow project at best, had — he proposed — to await the lessons war abroad would teach. As late as September, 1915, months after the sinking of the *Lusitania* had brought to Washington a sense of the imminence of war, Wilson saw no need "to stir the nation up in favor of national defense." Reflecting his enduring hope for peace, his position coincided with the views of most Americans, especially the liberals and agrarians, who cherished still their proud suspicion of all things military.

But others differed. Such episodes as the landing at Veracruz, such doctrines as strict accountability, suggested to men familiar with military matters the need to begin to prepare for war, so obviously a possibility. While Wilson was still, others, not just militarists, began to educate their countrymen. Foremost of these was Theodore Roosevelt, whose incessant alarms, justified but over-strident, doubtless roused more people than they frightened. He was joined during 1915 by a growing number of distinguished public figures, including Lindley M. Garrison, the incumbent Secretary of War, and three of his prominent predecessors. By summer of that year Tumulty and House were also beseeching Wilson to advocate preparedness. As the year wore on and he failed to speak out, many Democrats feared that on preparedness the Republicans would unite and win.

Only slowly so convinced, only reluctantly forced to face

the possibility of war, Wilson cautiously shifted his ground. In July he had instructed the armed services to formulate plans for expansion; in November, asking for far less than his experts said they needed, he recommended the training of a volunteer army of 400,000 citizen-soldiers who were to serve only a few months in each of several years. The inadequacy of this first public proposal by the President appalled Roosevelt. But Claude Kitchin, Democratic chairman of the House Ways and Means Committee, speaking the spirit of Bryan on the Hill, thought that Wilson's program would "shock the civilized world." Like so many of his colleagues, Kitchin objected equally strongly to strict accountability and the means to make it strict. Wilson's long silence about preparedness had permitted such a spread and such a hardening of antipreparedness attitudes within his party and across the nation that when he came at late last to his task, neither Congress nor the country was amenable to much persuasion.

Nevertheless, on a trip that carried him halfway across the continent, the President took his case to his constituency. "Let no man dare to say . . . that the question of preparation . . . is a question of war or of peace," he admonished, adding, however, it might be necessary "to use . . . force . . . to vindicate the right of American citizens everywhere to enjoy the protection of international law, . . . to sell . . . in the open neutral markets of the world." Peace, he had to admit, depended upon any "reckless commander of a submarine" whose private interpretation of what his government wished him to do "might set the world on fire." But the submarine, he confessed at last, was not the only threat to peace. War could come to the Americas as it had to Belgium. "Guarantors of the rights of national sovereignty . . . on this side of the water," vulnerable along the Atlantic coast, where most munitions were manufactured, the United States needed a force of men who could prevent an initial disaster and "a navy second to none." Peace, he now told his audiences, "depends upon the aroused passion of other nations and not upon the motives of the United States."

And it did; but this message, so recently incomprehensible to Wilson, now failed to reach any significant number outside of those who shared already his new point of view. To the limited tolerances of his restive fellow Democrats in Congress he therefore had to concede. They won their first victory when he rejected Secretary Garrison's plan to create a large reserve under the control of the regular army; they won their second when, after Garrison resigned, Wilson appointed in his place Newton D. Baker, a progressive whose antimilitarism matched that of Josephus Daniels, still civilian chieftain of the Navy; they won their third when Wilson and Baker accepted as a substitute for Garrison's program one formulated by the lobby of the National Guard and sponsored by Southern agrarians. This scheme, embodied in a bill the House of Representatives passed, provided only for "federalizing" the Guard by giving the War Department increased but still incomplete control over state units. The Senate, however, less infected by ruralism and less frightened by the prospect of centralizing military authority, rewrote the bill, modeling it closely on Garrison's specifications.

This gave Wilson a familiar role to play, and once again he played it well. Working out a compromise, he brought to bear upon the House continuing pressure in its behalf. Enacted in May, 1916, it doubled the regular army and gave to the War Department more authority than had the earlier House bill. The President's influence also helped the big-navy advocates, strong in the Senate but weak in the House, to carry their measure accelerating the building program, now redesigned to provide a "navy second to none." The agrarians also scored, however, by substituting new taxes for the administration's revenue proposals, including higher surtaxes and an inheritance tax, which made those most able to pay pick up the bill for preparedness.

Wilson accepted the tax law in the spirit of his timely, precampaign progressivism. But the mystique of optimistic liberalism, one main source of the progressive faith, had already won a larger triumph, expensive for the whole people, by so long postponing the President's adoption of a military program. He finally helped Congress accomplish more than Congress might have achieved without him, but the expansion of the navy had been dangerously delayed and the remodeling of the army was, according to professional standards, only a gesture. Tied to traditional attitudes toward national defense, unwilling for many months to consider how American security would be affected by a failure of his neutrality policy, the President gave almost no thought to the military problems of fighting a war in Europe, the battleground on which America would have to be defended. Nevertheless, his plans, satisfying the mass of Americans, eliminated preparedness as a party issue in 1916.

Wilson had adjusted himself nicely to the temper of the time. Although the Republicans, reassimilating the Progressives, nominated a moderate liberal, Charles Evans Hughes, the President had sufficiently appeased the Democratic left to claim progressivism for his own. Although Roosevelt, stumping for Hughes, made "Americanism" his leitmotiv, Wilson, diminuendo, played moving variations on that theme. While the most self-conscious Irish- and German-Americans embarrassed Hughes by supporting him openly, the most self-conscious white, Protestant, un-hyphenated Americans could, unembarrassed, vote for Wilson. Most of all, the Republicans suffered from Wilson's decision to make his canvass a campaign for peace.

This was in a sense disingenuous, for by Wilson's own account the chance of war lay in the hands of any reckless submarine commander. It was certainly deluding, for the *Sussex* pledge contained the potential for its own reversal. Yet in a larger sense it was Wilson who was deluded, confused by his continuing hopes for peace, by his interpretations of the war, and by those intuitions that directed him to the positions that the people preferred. In campaigning, as he did, as a guarantor of peace, he lived a myth in which he needed desperately to believe.

The myth developed when the Democratic keynoter at the national convention found the delegates spontaneously jubilant because, in spite of recurrent crises, "we did not go to war." As the Republicans increasingly criticized Wilson's Mexican and neutrality policies, as Roosevelt sounded more and more bellicose, as Hughes explained that he would have been tougher with Germany than Wilson had been, the President preached peace. "There is," he warned, "only one choice as against peace, and that is war. . . . A very great body of the supporters of that party outspokenly declare that they want war, so that the certain prospect of the success of the Republican Party is that we shall be drawn . . . into . . . the European war." By contrast, he explained, "I am not expecting this country to get into war." Bryan, minister plenipotentiary of peace, took Wilson's message through the West. Throughout

October the Democrats advertised: "He kept us out of war." In November their copywriters promised more: "Wilson and Peace with Honor? or Hughes with Roosevelt and War?"

Charmed by peace and progressivism, rural America voted for Wilson. So, by and large, did labor, the liberals, the intellectuals — enough to provide, in spite of defections by urban Democrats, the margin of a narrow triumph. But the victory of Wilson was not necessarily a victory for peace, for already the British had tightened regulations for neutral trade and the Germans had intensified their submarine campaign against the Allies. Troubled by the resulting tenseness in Anglo-American relations and the enlarged possibility of war with Germany, Wilson sought to follow the mandate for which he had asked by pressing immediately his efforts to arrange a negotiated peace. Clearly the war could not much longer be contained; he had either to terminate it or to sacrifice peace or honor or the two.

This much he planned to say in a note to the belligerent and the neutral powers of Europe. To end the "war of exhaustion and attrition," to enforce peace and keep the future secure, he was ready to pledge the "whole force" of the United States. He had clearly in mind already the concept of a league of nations, an international political association constructed to preserve peace by substituting a world parliament and law for force. Not his originally, this concept nevertheless became distinctly his. He had also in mind, furthermore, what was more immediately important. Planning as he was to ask from each warring side "a concrete definition" of the guarantees and objectives for which it fought, and to demand an immediate conference to make peace, he intended to direct American policy so as by strong pressure short of war to assist that side disposed more reasonably to negotiate.

Briefly the President was encouraged. Although the British had let their most recent talks with the Americans about ending the war come to nothing, the Germans had asked Wilson to take the initiative for peace. While he delayed, still musing about the form and the timing of his note, the German chancellor on December 12, 1916, announced his government's readiness to negotiate with its enemies. But behind this offer, superficially so cheering, brooded a militant and corrupted spirit. As this slowly became clear, Wilson's hopes expired.

The Germans had made their gesture not in weakness, not with humanitarian intent, but with confidence in their own impending victory. Masters of the eastern front, they expected, if the Allies rejected their terms, to smash France and Britain in the west. They had already decided, in the event negotiations failed, to resume unrestricted submarine warfare, risking American hostility in order to harass the British lines of supply. The conditions they had secretly in mind, moreover, asked the Allies in effect to surrender, to cede territory along the Baltic, in the Congo, in Belgium, France and Luxembourg.

Further communication disclosed this arrogance. Taking advantage of the German offer, Wilson dispatched a modified form of the note he had been planning. No government would reply to its request for a definition of purpose. The Germans instead called for a conference among belligerents. They expressed their willingness to join with the United States in creating an international organization after the conference, but they wanted no neutral involved in determining the terms of peace. Yet Wilson knew those terms concerned the neutrals. The Allies, replying publicly to the President's note, rejected out of hand the German proposal for a conference and demanded instead indemnities from Germany and the destruction of her power. But this was propaganda, for privately the British let Wilson know that they would discuss peace if the German terms were reasonable. Even before learning this, Wilson had tried to pin the Germans down. He would help, he informed them, to bring the Allies to accept a settlement re-establishing the *status quo ante*, creating a league of nations, and envisioning disarmament. On January 31, 1917, in only slightly moderated form, the Germans finally revealed their grasping terms. They also announced their submarines would sink on sight all ships, neutral or belligerent, in the eastern Atlantic and in the Mediterranean. At last, stripped even of his own roseate illusions, Wilson could not escape the world as it had become.

Still for a while he tried. As late as January 22, 1917, speaking, he felt, for "the silent mass of mankind everywhere," he had made a poignant address calling for peace at once and peace everlasting, for a league of nations, "peace among equals," "peace without victory." From his great pulpit he then reached again that vast congregation imbued, as was he, with a persisting faith in "the single supreme plan of peace, the revelation of our Lord and Saviour . . . [that] wars will never have any ending until men cease to hate." He spoke again a message of rational, Christian optimism, noble, inspired, revered. But also ironic, for while Germany remained powerful, there could be no peace without victory, and the terrible process of crushing Germany had already steeled her enemies against such a peace.

Nevertheless, suffused with his own message, Wilson

for several weeks after the German reply and the resumption of unrestricted submarine warfare would not admit to himself that war was his fortune. He did break relations with Germany, but he made no effort to hasten preparations for war; he would not use the navy to convoy merchantmen across the ocean; and he announced to Congress that he wished no conflict. He remained outwardly temperate even after learning on February 25 of the instructions of the German foreign minister, Alfred Zimmerman, to the minister in Mexico City, who was to propose, should Germany and the United States go to war, that Mexico join Germany and invite Japan to come along.

But if Wilson was not yet bellicose, he was committed still to his familiar interpretation of neutral rights. On that account he asked Congress for authority to arm merchant vessels and to employ any other methods necessary to protect American ships and citizens on the sea. Such latitude the agrarians would not grant. To convert them and their constituents, Wilson on March 1 released the Zimmerman note, which immediately provoked a wave of anti-German sentiment stronger, perhaps, than anything the President felt himself. The Democratic House nevertheless withheld from the bill it passed the broad authority Wilson wanted, and in the Senate a dozen antiwar progressives talked a stronger bill to death.

This "little group of willful men," as Wilson labeled them, struggled in vain, for the Zimmerman note had dissolved the mirage that the war was strictly European. The President on his own ordered the merchantmen armed, and German submarines on March 18 sank without warning three American ships. At this juncture, furthermore, the first Russian revolution established a limited monarchy, thereby ending for a brief season the despotism that had made Americans hesitate to join any cause with Russia, and Wilson learned authoritatively what England's friends had feared, that without American men, money and matériel the Allies would collapse. There could be no more hesitation. When all the cabinet, even Daniels, had recommended war, the President called Congress into special session.

Agonized by his decision, Wilson in the days that followed had to compose not just a war message, but himself. On April 1, in a moment of rare candor, he opened his secret heart to a friendly journalist: "He said war would overturn the world we had known . . . would mean that Germany would be . . . so badly beaten that there would be a dictated peace, a victorious peace. . . . He said . . . a war . . . required illiberalism at home to reinforce the men at the front." "The spirit of ruthless brutality," he predicted, would enter the very "fibre of our national life." But he could not see any alternative.

There was none. Wilson in the end decided for war because Germany forced him to. It had been Germany in 1914 that forced war upon France and Belgium. Whatever her grievances, she was bent on conquest. From this there was no immunity. Wilson had, to be sure, confused himself and his people by his tortured definitions of neutrality, but wiser definitions would not have changed the problem. For the United States there could be no real peace while aggression troubled Europe. Wiser definitions might, however, have helped Wilson and his countrymen understand their pass. As it was, in April, 1917, the disenchanted President saw before him only the dreadful prospect of the months ahead. Yet he had to ask Congress, as he did on April 2, to declare war.

He could no longer be deflected by his preference

for rational arrangements, for German policy destroyed
once and for all the optimistic expectations so long, so
stoutly challenged from divers quarters. As much as this
the President admitted to a journalist. But he could not
bring himself to say this to the nation. His war message
rehearsed perforce the story of the submarines, of sabotage and Zimmerman. It also reasserted that translucent
identity of law and justice which from the first sustained
the President's concepts of neutrality. Characteristically
Wilson personalized, attributing guilt not to the German
people but to their rulers. Characteristically he moralized.
Surely his splendid prose enveloped hopes he privately
found difficult to sustain. "It is," he said, "a fearful thing
to lead this great peaceful people into war, into the most
terrible . . . of all wars, civilization itself seeming to
hang in the balance. But the right is more precious than
peace, and we shall fight for the things which we have
always carried nearest our hearts, — for democracy, . . .
for the rights and liberties of small nations, for a universal
dominion of right by such a concert of free peoples as shall
bring peace and safety to all nations and make the world
itself at last free."

But if Wilson buried his doubts, what choice did he
have? How else was he to act, how else to lead? And if he
momentarily had suspected that a righteous peace was impossible, he nevertheless believed, as in every crisis he
always had, that his antagonist had sinned and sin had to
be punished, indeed liquidated. He believed, also as always, in parliaments, therefore in the ability of an international parliament after hostilities to order peacefully
and perceptively the affairs of the world. So at once he
doubted and he could not doubt, for it was part of him
to believe in the right and in his capacity to find and

pursue it. His peroration doubtless indulged fantastic
dreams, misled again a people already groping. It ignored
the real politics of international affairs; it complicated
peace making when the time to make peace came. But it
was also a glorious peroration, for in spite of the presence
in all human affairs of power and hate and greed, indeed,
resisting that presence, there endure attributes of mind
and soul that generate faith and love. However Wilson
erred, he put in persuasive form a message that through
many awful months of war sustained the compassionate,
the cheerful and the brave. Whatever it ignored, it gave
to Wilson as to other men the courage to confront their
tribulations, the promise — after trial — of new freedom.

V I I

A People's War

1917-1918

WILSON HAD SOWED neutrality and peace but harvested war. He predicated a human nature rational, moral and devout, but war brought out the bestial in man. He was alarmed by the potentialities for bureaucratic irresponsibility and aggrandizement in concentrations of economic or public power, but war made these concentrations indispensable. Indeed, by the attitudes it bred, the destruction it caused, the enormous, integrated productive efforts it demanded, modern total war denied the presumptions about the universality of enlightened gentility and about the beneficence of mechanistic competition upon which Wilson's concepts of democracy depended. The very necessity of bending to war's unwelcome insistencies made him believe with frenetic intensity that its end would justify its means. He came gradually to employ concentrations of authority and to indulge debaucheries of spirit tolerable to him only because of his now urgent, now wistful faith that out of war would emerge a Utopia of remembered yesterdays that never were — a brave, new world. For Wilson and the thousands who agreed with him, it had to be a war to end war, a war to make the world safe for democracy, a people's war — and "woe be to the man . . . that seeks to stand in our way in this day of high resolution when every principle we hold dearest is to be vindicated and made secure."

Because the nation was unprepared for waging war in Europe, the mobilization of military, economic and emotional resources was confused and painful. But fortunately the incomparable plenty of the United States compensated for its unreadiness. Fortunately also Wilson, after a faltering start, learned from the exigencies of war to give to the organization of the nation a steady direction. The reports of the war missions sent to the United States by England and France dissolved the President's hope that American money and matériel would alone provide the stuff of victory. These, to be sure, were needed; but the Allies needed also and urgently a large, equipped, well-trained American army. Yet the country lacked not only the army but the plans and facilities to raise it, the artillery, tanks and airplanes to arm it, the ships to transport it, even the tools to produce these necessaries.

Recognizing the inadequacy of his earlier plans, Wilson had quickly to overcome the persisting illusion of so many Americans that war was either a conspiracy of bankers sedulously to be resisted or a romantic challenge which sacrifice could master. A combination of these attitudes, reinforced by the tradition of voluntary military service, impeded the enactment of the selective service bill which the army had drafted. Two powerful Democrats, the Speaker of the House and the chairman of the House Committee on Military Affairs, opposed the bill. Southern Democrats raised the draft age from nineteen through twenty-five, recommended by the army, to twenty-one

through thirty, a range more attractive to mothers. To
protect the measure from his party in the House, the President had to rely upon Republican leadership and Republican votes. In the Senate, where the parties resumed their
normal roles, the contest turned on the sentimental issue
of whether Wilson should be forced to accept the volunteer division Theodore Roosevelt had offered to raise and
command. Roosevelt believed, as did his supporters, that
even if his troops went to France half trained, they would
arrive long before any other Americans and make up in
dash for what they lacked in experience. But the officers
Roosevelt had tentatively recruited were needed to staff
the divisions yet to be drafted, and Roosevelt himself,
stout, elderly, blind in one eye, had no knowledge of war
in the trenches. Nevertheless the Republicans in the Senate forsook their attempt to make Wilson swallow Roosevelt whole only after three weeks of debate had too long
delayed essential legislation.

Left free to dispose of volunteer units as he saw fit,
Wilson rejected them all, including Roosevelt's. More than
any other commander, the colonel could have dramatized
the war for the American people and dramatized American participation for the Allies. On these accounts the
French premier had wanted him to come. But World War
I was rather more a dirty than a dramatic war. The principle of conscription, furthermore, of leaving decisions
about the use of manpower to the military experts, had
firmly to be established. And even without Roosevelt's
division, Americans generated sufficient excitement about
the war; the operation of the draft produced no significant
opposition; and the drafted troops performed heroically.
The Yanks were slow in coming because conscription came
so late, but they arrived faster and in larger numbers than

the German general staff had thought they would. Over
a million soldiers reached Europe by the fall of 1918, providing there, just in time, the margin of manpower needed
to turn back the last German drive and to mount the offensive that brought victory.

If, perhaps, in Roosevelt's case Wilson was moved in
part by spite, he was nevertheless saved the embarrass-
ments of permitting politically ambitious soldiers high
command. Such was the saving also in the case of Major
General Leonard Wood, a talented organizer, a close
friend of Roosevelt, and a seeker of glory as much as of
service. General John J. Pershing, to whom Wilson had
entrusted the command of the American Expeditionary
Force, did not want Wood in Europe on any terms, for
any task. Wilson kept Wood home, and the laconic Pershing, dedicated to his difficult job, concentrated upon it
to the exclusion of political considerations.

Wilson rarely deviated from a reliance on his military
chiefs for the solution of military problems. The draft
produced a huge civilian army; the professionals directed
it. If the President never really understood them, much
less admired them, he left them pretty much alone. There
were times, to be sure, when Pershing wanted confidence
in some subordinate sent him, felt overlooked, or found
some new arrangement irritating. But on the whole "Black
Jack" had his quiet, stern and able way, preserving a freedom from interference from Washington, preserving also
— with Wilson's help and against French and British
wishes — the separate identity of the A.E.F.

The President, in spite of his innocence in naval matters, more directly troubled Admiral William S. Sims,
ranking American naval officer in Europe. Over Sims's informed objections Wilson insisted upon the costly mining

of the North Sea, an operation which probably missed its purpose of containing enemy submarines. He stood behind Sims, however, while the admiral overcame the resistance of British merchant captains to the organization of escorted convoys. Minimizing the risk from submarines, Sims's convoy system removed the single most pressing obstacle to fighting a transoceanic war.

Military command posed less of a problem than the command of the men behind the men behind the guns. Always wary of concentrations of authority, lacking precedents for economic mobilization, the President had to feel his way toward the creation of agencies sufficiently powerful to plan the production and distribution of the tools of war, to allocate to this end goods and services that otherwise were diverted into traditional but now frivolous civilian use. The absence of forehandedness made the task enormous. When war came, the army lacked data even on the uniforms and shoes it would need; neither military nor civilians had an inventory of resources or a plan for priorities. Consequently the first nine months of belligerency were given over largely to gaining an understanding of mobilization.

If Wilson began late and moved at first slowly, he moved continuously toward suitable arrangements. Over agriculture he first imposed the kind of control the entire economy was in time to feel. He had set up under Herbert Hoover a committee on food as a unit of the Council of National Defense, the diffuse planning agency established by the preparedness legislation of 1916. To enhance the authority of the committee, Wilson in the spring of 1917 asked Congress to endow him with power to control all phases of agricultural production and marketing. The House's Lever bill, amended though it was by a coalition of Republicans and agrarian Democrats in the Senate, accomplished this purpose. Wilson then created the Food Administration, where from first to last the exercise of power lay with Hoover. Relying largely on indirect controls and voluntary rationing, Hoover presided successfully over the expansion of American agriculture that alone made possible the feeding of the western nations fighting Germany.

The organization of industry took longer. To consolidate the loose authority of the Council of National Defense, Wilson in July, 1917, appointed under it the War Industries Board, empowered, with its subsidiaries, to pass upon American and Allied purchases, allocate raw materials and control production. Conflicts between the military services and the W.I.B. impaired its work for many months, but in March, 1918, Wilson rewrote its charter according to the specifications of Bernard Baruch, the board's new chairman. Concerned thereafter primarily with industrial priorities, the W.I.B. successfully eliminated bottlenecks, developed processes to reduce industrial waste, and guided new investment and the conversion of plants to essential work. Baruch's reorganization of the W.I.B. had its counterpart in the reorganization by Wilson and Secretary of War Baker of the general staff of the army. Establishing the now familiar "G" sections, Baker placed in charge of each experienced officers selected, without regard to seniority, for their demonstrated administrative abilities. Baker also recruited for the War Department new civilian talents, men who coordinated with their military associates the planning of the wartime economy.

As with industry, so with transportation and labor. Prewar arrangements failed under the stress of war. To permit effective routing of railroad traffic, increasingly snarled in spite of voluntary efforts among the roads to cooperate, Wilson asked for and received from Congress the authority to take over the railways. Secretary of the Treasury McAdoo, appointed Director General of the Railroads in December, 1917, exercised a control over transportation larger even than Baruch's over production. Rapidly McAdoo put his house in order, strengthening the financial position of the roads while he improved their services. As 1918 began, Wilson also unified the various agencies that had grown up for the common purpose of preventing labor disturbances. The War Labor Administration with its subsidiaries and affiliates ran a large, efficient conciliation service, standardized wages and hours, and registered and placed millions of laborers in war work. While keeping the country singularly free from serious strikes, the federal agencies protected labor from inequities which might otherwise have been imposed in the name of patriotism by a managerial group still hostile to labor leaders and their objectives. Indeed, during the war, while union membership increased dramatically, labor won shorter hours, higher wages and better working conditions.

As the duties of government in every sector of the economy multiplied, Wilson borrowed from industry scores of executives who transplanted in Washington techniques of management they had developed for Sears, Roebuck and Company, J. P. Morgan and Company, the Baltimore and Ohio Railroad, the United States Steel Corporation and similar concerns. Forced to bring bigness to government, the President brought with it its masters. He borrowed also their preferred form of organization, the corporation. Operating under latitudinarian state laws, corporations had a capacity for speed and flexibility of action far beyond what Congress permitted the ordinary bureau of the federal government. To gain these assets, Wilson created special corporations whose stock government officials voted for such divers purposes as building ships and controlling the price of sugar. Innovations such as these not only facilitated the prosecution of the war but also provided a model for economic mobilization to which government repaired during the great depression.

Yet Wilson's ultimate success, outstanding though it was, followed a number of failures which proceeded both from the inadequacy of national preparedness and from the rivalries that ordinarily infest large bureaucracies, especially in their formative period. Perhaps the worst experience was with aviation. So slow were American planners in designing an aircraft engine, so unready was the lumber industry for producing materials for airplanes, that American aviators had throughout the war to fly in British and French machines. The situation was almost as bad in the production of tanks and artillery, little better for coke. The shipbuilding program collapsed completely, forcing the government to rely for the transportation of troops and supplies upon bottoms seized from neutrals, purchased from private industry, or provided by the British.

In these and other cases, rumors of trouble circulated vigorously by the end of 1917. These derived dramatic credence in January, 1918, from an emergency order of the Fuel Administration, issued without warning, closing down vital industrial plants east of the Mississippi for four days. Obviously things were out of joint. The Senate Military Affairs Committee had already begun an investigation of the conduct of the war that was revealing all the growing pains of 1917. Its Democratic chairman now asserted publicly that the military establishment had fallen down because of waste and inefficiency in every bureau of the government. Theodore Roosevelt in a dozen different ways broadcast the same contention. Several worried Democratic senators and most Republicans supported a bill to create a war cabinet of three distinguished citizens which was, in effect, to exercise the powers Congress had conferred upon the President. Had this measure passed, Wilson would have become a figurehead.

He deserved a better fate, for by the time of the Senate's investigation, he had begun on his own to reorganize. And neither in 1917 nor later did any scandal taint the administration of the war. Yet the threat from the Senate did spur Wilson on. Admitting delays and disappointments, all — as he saw it — exaggerated by his critics, he praised the "extraordinary promptness and efficiency" with which his associates had executed tasks of "unparalleled magnitude and difficulty." To strengthen their position and his own, he prepared a bill giving him sweeping power to organize and manage all the executive agencies as he saw fit. Sponsored by Senator Overman, this measure passed both houses by large majorities in April, 1918. Although he used his new authority only sparingly, Wilson then completed the changes that made the record for 1918 first rate.

More than the vigilance of Congress, the maturing of the executive assured the mobilization of the economy for war. Congress obviously also matured, for in passing the Overman bill the Senate registered a tolerance of executive authority far larger than that of a year earlier when the Lever bill had met strong opposition. This tolerance in turn reflected the growing determination of the electorate to be on with the war, to accept the burdens and changes it imposed in order as expeditiously as possible to bring it to a victorious end. It must have been just this attitude that let Wilson design ever larger clusters of authority. Once the war was over, no one moved more rapidly than he to abolish them. Throughout the war, he retained his apprehensions about power in international affairs; he developed no real sympathy for industrialists or industrialism; he abandoned no part of his suspicion of "great organizations"; no part of his faith in the "pristine strength" of the old, individualistic America that the New Freedom had meant to restore. Only a faith as intense as his could fail to see that in the western world as it had become, what war demanded, peace in almost even measure would also need.

Not power itself, but anxiety empowered, during the war corrupted even Wilson's solicitude for the traditional liberties of English-speaking peoples. The President initiated or permitted developments that aggravated the emotions characteristic of a people at war. His first purposes were simply to educate his countrymen and to prevent aid to the enemy, but education and prevention degenerated to distortion and persecution.

So many Americans initially considered the war unnecessary, so many others were so unenthusiastic, that a week after war was declared Wilson created the Committee on Public Information to mobilize opinion. George Creel, chairman of the C.P.I., a Western journalist long identified with progressive causes, brought to his post experience, energy, and uncompromising self-assurance. He arranged with the working press a voluntary censorship that succeeded admirably at once in preventing the release of classified information and in keeping the American people reasonably well informed. He also called to his colors hundreds of artists and writers, who executed a campaign of propaganda without precedent in American history. They purveyed two major thoughts: one, the postulate of the President, that Americans fought only for freedom and democracy; the other, Creel's corollary, that the Germans, "Huns" all, were creatures of the devil attempting by the deliberate, lustful perpetration of atrocities to conquer the world. With only minor alterations Creel's version of the German soldier could have provided a splendid model for the SS troops of Hitler's time; in 1917 it represented mostly fantasy. At once reflecting and intensifying the unreasoning attitudes of men at war, the C.P.I. suggested daily that German spies had ears to every wall, German agents keys to every factory. Many of the releases of the committee carried antiunion overtones, more deliberately made German and suspect the political and economic ideas of the patriotic left. The propaganda of the C.P.I. helped sell bonds, combat absenteeism, reconcile some doubters to the war; but the price for this was large.

The national temper, of course, responded to other than just official stimuli. Especially among the syndicalist Industrial Workers of the World, there were some radicals whose violence had to be restrained. But there were many more demagogues, private agencies of propaganda, and self-appointed vigilantes who contributed, often with a calculated generosity, to the mounting national hysteria. Americans abandoned the teaching of the German language and the playing of great German music, abandoned also — as Wilson had predicted they would — tolerance and compassion. As their emotionalism grew, it was easily turned by clever men against Negroes, immigrants, even suffragettes, against all the objects of chronic American prejudices. The terror, before it subsided, reached heights unrivaled until the 1950's. To much of the sickness of attitude behind it, Americans had long been vulnerable; to some of that sickness, Wilson long insensitive. This insensitivity perhaps helps to explain his willingness officially to encourage emotions that absorbed persistent hates and fears. Creel, after all, was Wilson's agent; Creel's program of imposed conformity, his program.

Still stronger instruments for conformity were the various espionage and sedition laws the President endorsed. The Espionage Act of 1917 provided the authority the government needed to punish willful obstructionism, but in terms dangerously loose. The administration of the act fell to the provincial intelligences that permeated the Post Office and Justice Departments. These men closed the mails to publications whose only offense was socialism or an anti-British bias, prosecuted and convicted individuals who had done no more than criticize the Red Cross, the YMCA, or the financing of the war — men who had merely declared war contrary to the teachings of Christ. Wilson had originally asked for even larger powers of censorship; he continued to do so until two acts of Congress provided them. The Trading-with-the-Enemy Act of October, 1917, gave the myopic Postmaster General virtually unlimited authority over the foreign-language press; the Sedition Act of May, 1918, empowered the federal government to punish expressions of opinion which, regardless of their provable consequences, were "disloyal, profane, scurrilous or abusive" of the American form of government, flag or uniform. The recklessness of Congress in stocking such an arsenal against free speech had its source, surely, in the frenzy of the people; so also the timidity of the courts, where few judges elected to protect the freedoms the Constitution defined; and so also, though the President could have mitigated it, the execution of the laws. Of over fifteen hundred arrests, ten only were alleged to be for actual sabotage. Perhaps more than any other factor, this shocking record stimulated among men of good will an incipient disenchantment with Wilson.

The President turned his back on civil liberties not because he loved them less but because he loved his vision of eventual peace much more. To the neglect of other matters, he was preoccupied with the definition and articulation of war aims. That extraordinary concentration of intelligence and spirit which he lightly called his one-track mind focused on achieving possibilities that alone sustained his confidence in the decision to fight. Did the organization of government concentrate power beyond the limits he held safe? Did the conduct of government override the privacy and decency democracy demanded? No matter — there was coming a great day. So intensely did Wilson believe this, so determined was he to convince the people of the world, the American people included, that he had room within him for few other worries, tolerance for no conflicting evidence or thoughts.

Sentiment for a liberal peace was not original with Wilson. The substitution of an international comity for the alliance system, the substitution of arbitration for armaments, the institution among all peoples of self-government, the avoidance of the kinds of seizures and reparations that bred resentful vengeance, to all these enlightened men in Europe and America aspired. Especially in England and the United States, influential private organizations were engaged in making converts to these views. Wilson was something of a late comer. Not until 1916 did he publicly embrace the idea of a league of nations; not until a few months before the United States declared war did he begin assiduously to think about the components necessary for a peace without victory. Soon after war began he assigned the task of preparing detailed plans for peace to Colonel House and his staff of experts. The President himself assumed the more compatible task of persuasion.

Wilson's message derived its structure from the same premises that had underlain the New Freedom. Still making guilt personal, he asserted that the enemy was not the German people but their "military masters" who had "denied us the right to be neutral . . . filled our unsuspecting communities with vicious spies . . . sought by violence to destroy our industries." A necessary preliminary to any intelligent dealing with Germany, he later suggested, was the removal of the military party from authority there. He was teaching the Germans to elect good men. Wilson interpreted the war, furthermore, in one sense as a vast antitrust action against Germany. He intended to divest her of the power she had established over lands and peoples other than her own, to do so not only to permit these peoples the self-government they deserved but also to bring Germany down to manageable size. This accomplished and the military masters expelled, the Germans, like all other peoples, their hearts filled with the spirit of freedom, would — he presumed — participate as equals in the getting and spending of the world, join with other nations in an international parliament whose collective, democratic judgment would guard peace and plenty.

As he spoke, Wilson characteristically relied almost exclusively on the moral force of his position. If, gathering the fruits of the economics and political theory of his youth, he gave scant thought to the conditions that made plenty possible, if he miscalculated again the role of power in all affairs, if he overestimated the attraction to most people of Anglo-American political habits, he nevertheless restated in memorable language the presumptive faith of two centuries of democrats. "Peace," he said, "should rest upon the rights of peoples, not the rights of governments, — the rights of peoples great or small, weak or powerful, — their equal right to freedom and security and self-government and to a participation upon fair terms in the economic opportunities of the world." The grandeur of this message evoked everywhere glad expectations that out of war would be fashioned a peace so clean and just that the awful sadness of the war itself would not have been in vain. To his own spirit Wilson rallied his generation of Americans, convincing dirty, dying men that in death they earned their glory and their nation's. Of his faith the President made such a mighty power that in the end it tempered, as did nothing else, the proclivity of victors to seek only retribution.

Characteristically also, this magnificent leadership had no diplomatic sinews. Wilson made no effort before going to war to elicit Allied agreement to a liberal peace. By his choice the United States fought not as an Allied nation but as an associated belligerent, with the others but not of them. If Wilson thereby avoided the "entangling alliances" tradition forbade, he avoided also facing squarely the punitive intentions of the Allies which were recorded in the secret treaties governing their relationships. Though he must have known as early as April, 1917, about French and British designs for the division of German and Austrian possessions and the exaction of indemnities, he ignored these throughout the war, wishing away, as it were, the chief obstacles to his purpose. The freedom of the United States from any commitments to procure territory or reparations gave Wilson an open platform from which to educate; his own independence of the Allied leaders permitted him a boldness denied all captives of the secret treaties; but as he developed his plans for peace, he had absolutely no assurances that his associates in war would come along.

The President gave increasing specificity to his plans in a series of addresses delivered during 1918. Of the many points he made, some of them redundant, those that most captured the popular imagination were the basic fourteen he announced to Congress in January. A military and emotional crisis presented the occasion for this speech. The previous November the Bolsheviks had gained control of the government of Russia, had begun to arrange with Germany a separate and humiliating peace, and had begun also by terroristic methods to solidify their hold at home and advance their revolution elsewhere. To this latter end, successfully embarrassing the Allies, they released from Russian archives the imperialistic terms of the secret treaties between the Czarist government and the western powers. Both David Lloyd George, the British prime minister, and Wilson therefore felt compelled to reassert the commitment of the enemies of Germany to a just peace.

"We demand," the President explained, "that the world be made fit and safe to live in . . . safe . . . against force and selfish aggression. . . . The program of the world's peace . . . is our . . . only possible program." He then spelled out his Fourteen Points. Five were broad: open diplomacy, by which he meant not an end to private discussion but an end to secret agreements; free use of the seas in peace and in war; the reduction of armaments; the removal of economic barriers to free trade among nations;

an impartial adjustment of colonial claims. Eight points, all pertaining to specific territorial settlements, in common advanced the principle of self-determination. These looked to the German evacuation of Russian territory, the restoration of Belgian independence, the return to France of Alsace-Lorraine (Germany's by conquest since 1870), the erection of an independent Poland, and the autonomous development of each of the various peoples of Austria-Hungary and European Turkey. The fourteenth, crowning point called for the formation of "a general association of nations . . . under specific covenants for the purpose of affording mutual guarantees of political independence and territorial integrity to great and small states alike." Three days earlier Lloyd George had made all but the first three of Wilson's points, but Lloyd George had also advocated reparations, and Wilson's was both the broader program and the grander prose.

The Fourteen Points became a symbol of what Wilson stood for, of what he called "the moral climax of this . . . final war for human liberty." Yet they were unofficial, neither the public policy of the American government, of which the executive was only one part, nor the settled policy of the Allied governments, which had no hand in their formulation. They were also in places vague — self-determination, for example, could mean all things to all aspirant nations. They were in places contradictory — the boundaries of an independent Poland were sure to contain non-Polish peoples. They were in places at variance with inflexible national policies — the British had cultivated their navy deliberately to prevent free use of the seas in time of war. They were in places anathema to many Americans — those, for instance, who still cherished protective tariffs.

For the leaders of the Allies and for many of the American people the moral climax had not yet come. This became manifest in the fall of 1918, when the victorious course of western arms brought on negotiation of an armistice at just the time the calendar demanded congressional elections in the United States. The negotiation revealed latent but serious differences between Wilson and the Allied leaders; the campaign demonstrated that no single issue, certainly not Wilson's peace, could be disentangled from the complex of partisan national politics.

Before the Allied offensive had by September crippled the German armies, the dissemination by Allied and especially by American propagandists of Wilson's program for peace had begun to persuade influential Germans that they could expect justice from their enemies. Though the Allies would in time have been able to destroy the German forces, Wilson's pronouncements liquidated much of the German will to persevere. So did the negotiations which he undertook when on October 6, 1918, at the urging of the military, the new German chancellor addressed a note to him accepting the Fourteen Points as a basis for peace and proposing, on that condition, the arrangement of an armistice.

In the exchange of notes that followed, Wilson struck a posture sufficiently charitable to lead the Germans on, sufficiently firm to force them incontestably to admit defeat. This was not to entail unconditional surrender, but of all the chiefs of state and military commanders, only Pershing opposed terminating the war on the basis of satisfactory military guarantees. Exhausted by four years of attrition, the French and the British, determined though they were to win security, knew they needed peace. They recognized also that Bolshevism, surging westward on the

seas of devastation and despair, stood to gain the most
from continued fighting. Aware of all this, though he consulted none of his associates in war, Wilson also realized
that negotiation could hasten German surrender whereas
delay would consume scores more of American lives. But
neither these insights nor his charity made him, as the
Germans hoped they might, soft about his work.

Wilson from the first refused to consider proposing to
the Allies any cessation of arms unless German forces were
immediately withdrawn from all invaded territory. Re-
jecting a German counterproposal for a mixed commission
to supervise this evacuation, the President insisted that the
Germans provide "absolutely satisfactory . . . guarantees
of the maintenance of the present military supremacy
of the armies" of the Allies. He instructed them also to
cease at once their "wanton destruction" of cities and their
"illegal and inhumane" practices, including submarine
warfare. After the Germans acceded to these demands,
designed by Wilson as they were "to make a renewal of
hostilities on the part of Germany impossible," the President on October 23 informed them that he was sending
their appeal to discuss an armistice to the Allied governments. In the same note he made more explicit than he
had before the suggestion that reasonable terms would de-
pend upon the establishment in Germany of responsible,
democratic government. If the United States "must deal
with the military masters and the monarchical autocrats of
Germany now, or . . . later," he warned, "it must demand not peace negotiations, but surrender." Clearly the
prearmistice terms the President specified called upon the
Germans to accept both military defeat and the appurte-
nances, at least, of democracy.

Beyond this, the determination of the actual provisions

of armistice fell to the Allied leaders, who had never even acknowledged the existence of the Fourteen Points, the condition of the German suit. Indeed, when they sat down in Paris with Colonel House, who represented Wilson there, they disclaimed knowledge of what the Fourteen Points were. After House explained them, the British rejected the point on the freedom of the seas. The French demanded the Germans be informed reparations would be exacted for all civilian damage they had caused. Further alterations would have been made had not House twice suggested that if the Allies did not assent to the Fourteen Points, Wilson might arrange a separate peace with Germany. Wilson agreed to the French and British changes; they and the Italians withdrew with reluctance other acquisitive demands. But their reservations about the President's postulates postponed the definition of a consensus. This let the Germans expect more charity than their European enemies intended.

Yet the Allies had agreed upon enough to permit their supreme military commander to receive German representatives. The armistice they announced on November 11 pledged the western powers, with the changes noted, to make a peace based upon the Fourteen Points. Precisely what this meant only the future would tell. It also provided for the immediate German surrender of vast quantities of war materials, including the submarine fleet, and for the withdrawal of German forces not just from occupied territory but well beyond the east bank of the Rhine — conditions both precluding German renewal of the war and obliterating, as it worked out, German influence on the final terms of peace.

Large though this achievement was, Wilson's progress toward it engendered within the United States an excited opposition based largely on fractious partisanship. Both parties contributed to the involvement of peace in politics, as they did to the exploitation of every issue the war had raised. During the war the coalition of interests that was the Democratic party fell apart, while the Republicans, under the adroit management of Will Hays of Indiana, their masterful national chairman, rebuilt their strength upon the ruins. Too late and at too great a risk Wilson attempted to reverse this turn.

Republican criticism of the conduct of the war hurt the President and his party much less than did the voting record of those Southern Democrats in key congressional posts who had consistently obstructed such war legislation as the draft. Their policies, some progressive, some parochial, won the Republicans new friends. This was true of taxation. For the conservative bill of the administration, the Southern agrarians substituted their own. It imposed heavy, purposefully redistributive income, inheritance and excess-profits taxes, taxes designed to minimize the need for federal borrowing, to take the private profit out of war and incidentally out of the sections where most of the profit was being made. This equitable measure solidified the Republican hold upon the industrial East. So equally did the successful Southern support of wartime prohibition, anathema to most urban workers, Republican or Democrat, and especially to the Democratic machines, whose captains never forgave the rural evangelicals for the long thirst imposed upon them and their constituents. No less outraged were Western farmers, normally Republican but in 1916 a source of Democratic victory. Jealous of the price of wheat, which the Lever Act empowered Wilson to control, impatient when he would not raise the price, they particularly resented the inflated price of cotton which

Southern votes had spared from regulation. On this alone the Republicans could attract the vote west of the Mississippi.

So the coalition that had elected Wilson crumbled. The liberal fervor of 1912, the progressivism of 1916 had faded away, and with them the basis for success. In domestic policy, Wilson and the Democrats offered nothing particularly attractive to the middle-class American who felt his taxes were too high, to the farmer who considered the price of wheat too low, to the intellectual worried about civil liberties, to the urban worker deprived of beer and confronted with the draft. Only the South remained completely loyal to the party and its leader. But the South was not enough to win elections, especially in 1918, when Republican resurgence gained impetus from the weariness of people with meatless days and wheatless days, with manless homes — the weariness of war.

Northern Democratic leaders, recognizing their liabilities, concluded that they might retain control of Congress only if Wilson would endorse the Democratic candidates, endow them with his personal and presidential prestige. But Wilson, concentrating on global matters, more than ever impatient with local politics, had declared with gross inaccuracy that politics were adjourned. The Republican assault upon his foreign policy changed his mind.

As the negotiation of the armistice proceeded, the Republicans, exploiting the emotionalism of war, attacked the President's whole concept of peace without victory. Some had confidence only in an alliance system rebuilt to neutralize the Germans. Most, however, simply shared the sentiments of the many Americans who wanted unconditional surrender, the kaiser hanged, and Berlin invaded. While Wilson communicated with the Germans during

October, the critics of his intentions found a large audience responsive to Theodore Roosevelt's demand that peace be dictated by "hammering guns" rather than "clicking . . . typewriters."

This tactic had effect. Democratic leaders in Congress, the cabinet, and the national committee, many themselves obsessed with a hatred of all things German, urged the President to insist on drastic terms for an armistice, including the overthrow of the Hohenzollerns. Meeting them part way, Wilson made increasingly severe the tone of his notes to Germany. Yet his final posture, as one of his discerning counselors noted, though it might impress the thoughtful, could not elicit the enthusiasm the party needed. Only unconditional surrender could have accomplished this, and to his credit Wilson refused to let the exigencies of the election warp a policy he considered just and wise.

These exigencies did, however, persuade him to take a comparable risk. Late in October he yielded to continuing requests for a blanket endorsement of the Democratic ticket. In so doing, moreover, against the advice of the politicians urging him to act, he made his appeal to the voters turn on the question of his foreign policy. With obvious irritation, he also gave his request a sharply personal and partisan twist. "If you have approved of my leadership and wish me to continue to be your unembarrassed spokesman in affairs at home and abroad," he wrote on October 25, "I earnestly beg that you will express yourselves unmistakably to that effect by returning a Democratic majority to both the Senate and the House of Representatives. . . . The leaders of the minority . . . have unquestionably been pro war, but they have been anti-administration. . . . This is no time . . . for di-

vided counsel. . . . The return of a Republican majority
. . . would, moreover, certainly be interpreted on the
other side of the water as a repudiation of my leadership.
. . . If . . . it is your wish to sustain me, . . . I beg that
you will say so in a way which it will not be possible to
misunderstand."

This appeal for a Democratic Congress charged with
partisanship the very policies Wilson had need to protect
from irrelevant intrusions. It infuriated patriotic Republicans who had again and again supported war legislation.
It probably helped some Democratic candidates, but not
enough. The Republicans gained control of both houses of
Congress, though in the Senate by just one vote. They won
on no single issue, but Wilson had made much of affairs
abroad in his appeal, and the Republicans later found it
useful to claim that foreign policy determined the results.
By an interpretation he invited, though he knew the
American system could not yield a vote of confidence, Wilson stood repudiated five days before the armistice, just
when he needed to be strongest to defend his cherished
plans for peace against the hostile purpose of the Allies.

Wilson's decision to ask for a mandate for his policies, a
decision produced partly by his persisting vision of himself
in Gladstone's role, made him the victim of the tensions of
war that shaped the election of 1918. Tendencies he had
not tried to curb ensnared him. The official mobilization
of hatred, whetting phobias politicians both exploited and
endowed, fed the resistance to him and to his program.
Prejudices of which he had too long been unaware had begun to eat away his political support; one segment of his
party had so dominated the others that it destroyed his
surest source of strength. All this began before the war,
but war hastened the corruption of the spirit of democracy

and the disruption of the party that bore its name. The attention Wilson gave to his splendid international purpose was needed equally at home.

It was not in Wilson's power to provide it. He lost himself, as he had at times before, in a transcendent faith so dear to him he could not think that others did not partake of it. So it was when the fighting stopped. The hope he placed in the armistice overwhelmed the doubts the election might have raised. "God has in His good pleasure given us peace," he wrote. "It has not come as a mere cessation of arms, a mere relief from the strain and tragedy of war. It has come as a great triumph of right." He believed in the end just what he had believed at the beginning, just what he had to believe.

V I I I

The Only Disinterested Person

1918–1919

THE DISCHARGE of the duties of the Presidency created for the moralist an awkward problem. He was at once the keeper of a rigid conscience and the creature of a political system that worked only when he bent that conscience to conform to the narrow set of public tolerances. Great though it could be made, the power of his office carried him only so far; thereafter he had either to combine influence with compromise or, defending virtue, lose his way.

Something of this dilemma inhered in every executive position. Wilson at Princeton for a time made his sense of situation and persuasion the formidable implement of a serviceable ethic, but in the end obdurate certitude cost him his incisiveness and his goal. In higher office the pattern was the same. His ambitions, his obligations to his party controlled his conscious course far less than did the dictates of judicious conscience. Without offending his sensitive morality, he made his domestic reforms the expression of a common theme. Changes of mind there were, but not of heart.

So also in making foreign policy, self-searching more than self-seeking governed Wilson. His erratic course to war at every crossing took the turn marked by convictions confused but genuine. These, happily for him, impelled decisions continually acceptable to the moving national consensus. But under the best conditions this was a difficult step to keep. Wilson's was a nineteenth-century intelligence, obsolescing at a rapid rate, and this obsolescence the war accelerated. Conscience and intellect, stern, bright, intrinsically even dear, stood still while the race of time transfigured the world they understood. Fixed on its noble end, the one-track mind sensed less and less its growing isolation. Election day in 1918 left no impression. Increasingly thereafter conscience made a coward of resilience. The pace, already faltering, was broken. The President went one way, his Congress, his constituency, indeed his world, another, until he stood at last alone.

The stakes were so high, the difficulties so enormous, that perhaps no man could have escaped this denouement. The tragedy was not just Wilson's, but his times'. There were, as the final scenes unrolled, many actors, none heroes, and none really villains unless human frailty is counted villainous. In an abundant frailty Wilson shared. Yet, with unflagging courage, embroiled in a situation he was not built to master, he came so close to triumph that his failings nag where those of a lesser man might not be noticed. All this endowed the last acts of his career with an enduring passion.

With the signing of the armistice Wilson faced two inseparable tasks more taxing than any he had assumed before. To achieve the kind of peace he wanted, he had first to cope with the Allies — wounded, angry nations poised to satisfy ambitions multiplied by the grievances of war.

Whatever treaty he could arrange with them had next to command the votes of two thirds of the Senate, where the Republicans, determined to win again in 1920, had elected a majority. Much of what the Allies demanded, moreover, like much the President sought himself, excited the antagonism either of individual senators or of blocs of constituents they ordinarily appeased.

For what lay ahead the President needed deep resources of tact and elasticity and patience. Some of these he was to muster, but two presuppositions, long the staffs of his existence, depleted the necessary store. "In the name of the people of the United States," he declared, "I have uttered as the objects of this great war ideals, and nothing but ideals, and the war has been won by that inspiration." The British and the French could not concede this. Nor was it true, any more than was the tenet that most deluded him, the faith that "there is a great wind of moral force moving through the world, and every man who opposes . . . that wind will go down in disgrace."

Wilson's conviction that he was a special instrument of this moral force was the strongest of several considerations prompting his determination to go to Europe to participate in making peace. The pending settlements, as he said, were of "transcendent importance" to the world, sufficient cause for a President's then unprecedented departure from the United States upon a diplomatic mission. There were outstanding problems of reconversion from war, but Wilson referred some of these to the states, some — like the future of the railroads — to Congress, declining even to offer a judgment of his own. Most of the rest, he believed, needed no attention. "Our people," he asserted, "do not wait to be . . . led. They know their own business, are quick . . . at every readjustment." In the few weeks following the armistice he liquidated the complex apparatus constructed to guide the economy during war. His haste, common to men of both parties in Washington, relinquished to private business power over production, prices and employment that soon subjected the entire people to severe, unnecessary economic maladjustments. But the President's confidence in the mechanism of the market place prevented him from foreseeing this and left him free to concentrate, as his heart compelled him to, on international affairs. Whatever he neglected, his sense of duty, the priority of his undertaking, ultimately his performance at the council table, all supported his decision to go abroad.

There was little to support his choice of associates. He selected neither any member of the Senate, whose consent to the treaty might have been readier had one of its own helped frame it, nor any active member of the Republican party, whose partisan sensitivities were swelled by this omission. The President could not forgive the Republicans their attacks on his foreign policy during the recent campaign; he could countenance not even mild dissent from the plan he had in mind; he had never been able to work effectively with men whose stature rivaled his own, and now particularly he felt the mission he began had to be peculiarly his. In his most tolerant humor he would have rejected the incoming Republican chairman of the Senate Foreign Relations Committee, Henry Cabot Lodge, for many years his acid critic, an intractable Tory, an intimate of Roosevelt. But, against the wise advice of several counselors, he also passed over the best qualified Republican statesman, Elihu Root, sometime Secretary of State under Roosevelt, former Senator from New York, renowned authority on international law and arbitration.

Another eligible, ex-President Taft, unlike Root a public advocate of an international league to enforce peace, likewise failed to win the President's approval. Those who were appointed impressed Wilson's political opponents as at best unrepresentative and at worst sycophantic. This was essentially the case, for Wilson settled upon delegates from whom he expected informed but pliant cooperation: Secretary of State Lansing, whose office could not be overlooked though his advice, in Wilson's view too legalistic, was largely disregarded; Colonel House, whose attachment to the President's program was thought to be complete; Henry White, a veteran, patrician career diplomat, titularly a Republican, quiet, respected, but uninfluential; and General Tasker H. Bliss, a military expert endowed with broad talents valuable but unpublicized.

The President disdained public opinion as well as politics. Only the newspapers could continuously interpret his negotiations in Europe to the American people; he had, as he knew, no facility in dealing with the press; but for his official press representative in Paris he chose George Creel, whose wartime work had seemed to many journalists a form of censorship. Wilson had to agree, furthermore, to holding the important meetings of the conference in secret. This disturbed the journalists, who had mistakenly assumed that open diplomacy meant public negotiation. Unwilling to discuss his unsuccessful opposition to the secrecy imposed, Wilson further alienated the press by making consistently uninformative his official news releases. He simply saw no need to explain or justify himself. "Tell me what's right," he had urged the impressive group of experts who accompanied the American delegation, "and I'll fight for it." There was, he thought, some right, some right he would win, some right the gale of moral force drove irresistibly before him.

Men everywhere, he presumed, held his ideals. As he traveled through Europe during the interval between his arrival there and the beginning of the conference, he was acclaimed by crowds in France, Italy and England as no man had been for decades. They saw in him a symbol of American aid, of the end of the war, of the prospect of their national ambitions. But he took their greeting to signify complete accord with his objectives. Incautiously he neglected both clarity and grace. Speaking to the French of his indignation over the ruin wrought by the armies of the Central Powers, of his desire to meet just punishment, he let them think this meant their fierce determination to dismember Germany. Deaf to the prompting of Lloyd George, he did not bother to acknowledge British sacrifices. Again he saw no need to. He embodied, he told the British, the spirit of a great nation. Privately he maintained that while other nations shared this spirit, their leaders failed to represent it. It fell to the Americans, therefore, "the only disinterested people at the Peace Conference," and particularly to him, to translate the transcendent good into the articles of a treaty.

Wilson never expected every detail of the settlement to harmonize immediately with perfect justice. Indeed he never attributed to the Fourteen Points — the body of the armistice agreement with Germany — that characteristic. Rather, he had in mind three levels of objectives. The Fourteen Points provided the guides to his smallest concerns, the specific geographic, ethnographic, economic and military arrangements, which he realized would contain many imperfections. "I am not hopeful," he stated, "that the individual items of the settlement . . . will be altogether satisfactory . . . no man and no body of men . . . know just how." "Yet if we are to make unsatisfactory settlements," he continued, "we must see to it that they are rendered more and more satisfactory." This larger objective, the first purpose of his negotiations, he intended to achieve by the establishment of a league of nations which was over the years to preserve the peace by continuously adjusting its initial specifications. The settlements might be temporary, he told the first plenary session of the conference, "but the action of the nations in the interest of peace and justice must be permanent." The league was to embody permanent processes for action, and more — his largest purpose — the prompt organization not of nations only but of "the moral force of the world."

But the world was terribly sick, and, except for Wilson, each doctor at Paris cared not for saving its soul but for protecting the particular organ of which he had made a specialty. War had depleted the economic and human resources of every great power except the United States. It had precipitated the Bolshevik revolution in Russia, and the revolution in turn made her unwanted and unrepresented at the conference, brooding and dissatisfied with its designs. Spreading in the wake of war, the pestilence of Communism threatened permanently to infect all Russia's neighbors. Austria-Hungary had simply ceased to be. Where it had been, the quarrels of self-generated self-determination, complicated by revolution, were forging in malice the states which were to speckle the map of central and eastern Europe whether the men at Paris willed it or not. Germany's new republican government, born in the defeat of her arms, had to face revolution at the borders, Red plots within, and a populace increasingly exasperated by a shortage of foodstuffs perpetuated by the continuing Allied blockade. In Siberia, American, British and Japanese troops, engaged officially in supporting a disintegrating White Russian resistance, unofficially watched each other's plans for eastern Asia. To organize this world, much less its moral force, was an unpropitious venture.

The peacemakers, moreover, represented particularistic, even centrifugal intentions. For his country Wilson sought neither territory nor indemnities; not so his talented adversaries from the four other major powers. There was Orlando of Italy, a gentleman of culture, a learned lawyer, a friend of the idea of a league of nations, but first and always the inflexible spokesman of his country's territorial demands. There was Baron Makino of Japan, deliberately inscrutable, unconcerned about European problems, a resourceful bargainer determined Japan should hold what she had taken from Germany and also get title from the conference for these holdings.

Above all there were Lloyd George of England and Clemenceau of France. Gifted with a telepathic intuition about people, Lloyd George was affable but shifty. Probably better than any rival at the conference he understood the twentieth century; but he had little interest in mastering detail, and his partially informed intelligence yielded with continual ease to his political ambitions. He had fixed his sights to protect, where possible to expand, the British Empire and British primacy in trade and on the sea. He had, moreover, just won a national election after a campaign during which he and his party courted the electorate by promising to squeeze the Germans dry for reparations.

Fighter though he was, Lloyd George was not as tough

as France's "Tiger," Clemenceau — not as old or tired, as cynical or tenacious, as acid or alone. Clemenceau, Lord Keynes once wrote, "had one illusion — France; and one disillusion — mankind, including Frenchmen, and his colleagues not the least." He had two intertwined objectives, revenge and French security. These, as he saw it, entailed the absolute destruction of German power, existing or potential. Clemenceau, Lloyd George, Makino and Orlando consulted traditional canons of national self-interest above which Wilson thought the world could rise. Each knew precisely what he wanted, whereas the President's ultimate purpose was intangible. Each, though Wilson could not believe it, represented the temper of his own countrymen, while the President increasingly did not.

Nor was this all. The President's antagonists were bound by the terms of the various treaties among their nations to support most of each other's claims. More important still, their armies held most of the territories they planned to annex or to assign. France's Marshal Foch commanded the troops, some Allied, some French, in Alsace-Lorraine, the Rhineland and the Ruhr; the British and the Dominions camped in former German colonies in Africa and the islands of the South Pacific; the Japanese, where German flags had flown in the central Pacific and Shantung; the Italians, in Trentino and the Tyrol and, before the conference adjourned, in the contested port of Fiume. Principles of justice or self-determination weighed light against the fact of possession, in international real estate nine tenths of the effective law. Against these odds, the wonder was that Wilson accomplished anything. A less persistent, less inspired man could not have won what he extracted from the strength of his reluctant peers. At times he stumbled. At times he gave way to the strain of being incessantly disagreeable to a small company of men. But in decision after decision, his perseverant influence made its mark.

The first major problem to which the conference turned was the disposition of German colonies. The Fourteen Points called for an impartial settlement of all colonial claims, giving equal attention to "the interests of the populations concerned" and the "equitable" case of the government whose title was to be determined. The Germans interpreted this to guarantee at least some protection for their titles in Africa and the Pacific. But Wilson and his associates in war, convinced as they were that Germany's rule had been oppressive, resolved to divest her of her colonies. To estop imperialism, the President hoped to make small neutrals like Switzerland and Sweden guardians for the League of Nations of the colonies which, under trusteeship, were to move toward independence. His scheme had the additional attraction of creating for the League an important job. There was, however, no possibility of British or Japanese surrender of territory taken during hostilities. The secret treaty between Japan and England expressly granted the German islands in the Pacific north of the equator to Japan, south of that line to Australia and New Zealand. The recipients looked upon these as essential to their national defense. So it was also in Africa, where the South Africans only with pain had conquered their German neighbors. Nevertheless Wilson prevented outright transfers, persuading the Allies to settle instead for "mandates" similar to those he had intended for the Swiss. These obliged their holders to render to the League annual accountings of their administration, to help subject peoples in areas such as Mesopotamia to stand alone, to protect those in places like Central

Africa from traffic in slaves and arms and liquor. The compromise left the Japanese and British with what Lloyd George considered a pocketful of territory, but under some surveillance. This was in itself without precedent. The imperfections in the mandate system, moreover, the President hoped the League would gradually correct.

Simultaneously with his discussions of the colonial question, Wilson had steered his draft of a covenant through the commission of the convention organized to prepare a plan for a league. Here, too, he encountered opposition. The French wanted not an international association to preserve peace but a military alliance to contain Germany. The Japanese, amenable to a league, complicated negotiations by proposing, partly for trading purposes, the inclusion of a statement of racial equality pledging member nations not to discrimintate against the nationals of other members. To this the Australians were more hostile even than their fellow racists in the United States. But the Italians, pleased by the President's endorsement of the northern boundary they desired, cooperated with him; and the British, enjoying as they did much of his confidence in constitutional devices, gave him continually their more important support. Gracefully the Japanese, their point made, let their mandates temporarily assuage their pride. With much more obvious irritation the French also succumbed to Anglo-American pressure, but only after the President modified his proposal so as not to preclude the realization of their objectives elsewhere in the treaty. Wilson in turn accepted within the charter evasions on the issue of disarmament, which some of the British and Americans held as necessary as did the French. His own vision of using the League to oppose aggression — though he had in mind moral rather than military preventives —

suited the French purpose to enlist any available weapon against the possibility of Germany's marching again. Unanimously the commission in mid-February, 1919, approved a covenant substantially similar to what Wilson had drafted, a document, Wilson reported to the conference, with "a pulse of sympathy in it . . . a compulsion of conscience throughout it."

League

The Covenant established mechanisms and defined procedures characteristically Wilsonian, products obviously of his youthful adventures with parliaments and constitutions. Signatories of the treaty, of which the Covenant was a part, were each to be represented by one vote in the Body of Delegates. Larger power rested in the Executive Council, which was to consist of representatives of the United States, the British Empire, France, Italy and Japan, and of four other states selected by the Body of Delegates. Decisions of the council required unanimity of its membership except in those cases where a member was party to a dispute. The Covenant also established a permanent secretariat, a permanent international Bureau of Labor, and the mandate system; it included articles providing for the publication of all treaties entered into by its members, for the admission of new members by a two-thirds vote of the delegates, and for amendment by a three-fourths vote. For the keeping of peace, its central purpose, the Covenant obliged signatories before resorting to war to submit disputes either to inquiry by the council or to arbitration by a Permanent Court of International Justice which the council was to establish. Breach of this article, by definition an act of war against all members of the League, was to be punished by the severance of economic relations with the offending state. In such cases, though the League had no armed force, the council could recommend what military and naval units each member should contribute for the protection of the League and its principles. The council, furthermore, was to advise upon the means to satisfy the obligations of Article X, in Wilson's view the heart of the charter, which bound signatories "to respect and preserve as against external aggression the territorial integrity and . . . political independence of all . . . members of the League."

This was, as Wilson said, a very simple document. It did not create a superstate, for the requirement of unanimity in the Executive Council protected the national sovereignty of each major power. The same requirement stood between the League and any assurance that it might have the physical force to sustain its decisions. Its deliberations, moreover, would fail to reflect a full consensus of significant nationalities until the victorious powers should choose to invite Germany and Russia to membership. But the Covenant did create the first meaningful international organization in modern history. It had the potential with time and trial to implement both peace and justice. And it fulfilled the President's wise intentions to recognize war and the threat of war as everybody's business and to provide a forum for their discussion. "We are," he explained, "depending primarily . . . upon one great force, . . . the moral force of the public opinion of the world — the cleansing and clarifying and compelling influences of publicity — so that intrigues can no longer have their coverts, so that designs that are sinister can . . . be drawn into the open, so that those things . . . may be properly destroyed by the overwhelming light . . . of the condemnation of the world."

The sense of achievement Wilson expressed when he read the Covenant to the conference marked, though he did not then suspect it, a summit in his negotiations. After the reading he made a brief trip to the United States to attend to unavoidable domestic chores before resuming his work at Paris. At home he encountered directly the dangerous opposition to his League which, in his absence, the Republican leadership had been organizing. The essence of this opposition was partisanship, but it had other fertile sources. Those German- and Irish-Americans who had been unreconciled to the war itself remained hostile to any handiwork of the President and the Allies. To the Irish, who urged him to make home rule for Ireland a condition of peace, Wilson was not polite, much less sympathetic. He was cold also toward those sincere and influential lawyers who held the hardened belief that the best hope of peace was not a world parliament but international law interpreted by an international court. Not lawyers only but many other Americans also hesitated to depart from national tradition to the extent they felt the President had. They thought of their past as having been sterilized from the Old World; they thought of the Monroe Doctrine as a kind of inoculation against European war and European woe; they thought of the Covenant as an "entangling alliance," a departure from safety as well as from tradition. These confusions, breeding widespread susceptibility to the propaganda of Wilson's opponents, made necessary dispassionate explanations to the public and measured concessions to the Senate which the President remained reluctant to provide.

The developing conflict flared on March 4, 1919, Wilson's last day in the United States. Henry Cabot Lodge then produced a round robin, signed by thirty-seven Republican senators, four more than were needed to defeat the treaty. Describing the Covenant as unacceptable in the form it had been written, this called upon the conference to defer the consideration of a league until after peace was made. Wilson spoke that night at the Metropolitan Opera House in New York. His audience was receptive, but in the wings a delegation of Irish-American agitators awaited him with threatening incivility. At his side was Taft, representing the League to Enforce Peace, a friendly organization, but Elihu Root had declined an invitation to attend. Wilson, electing to interpret Taft's presence to mean the League was not a partisan issue, went on in a manner so sanctimonious, so assured that Taft was stunned. Asserting that nothing in America had to be explained to him, the President condemned the "careful selfishness" of his critics, their "comprehensive ignorance of the state of the world" and of the "rush of spirit" sponsoring the League. This gave the appearance of partisan stubbornness to his central theme, his announcement that when the treaty came back "gentlemen on this side will find the Covenant not only in it, but so many threads of the treaty tied to the covenant that you cannot dissect the covenant from the treaty without destroying the whole vital structure." This was accurate. The interrelationship, moreover, was essential for the working out of problems still before the conference. But the President's unwarranted manner irrevocably associated uncolored fact with the controverted merit of his own judgment.

Though Wilson would not consider separating the Covenant from the treaty, his sojourn in the United States did convince him that he had to bow to the major demands of his reasonable critics in and out of the Senate. Taft, whose counsel he now solicited, helped persuade him to introduce four revisions to the Covenant on which the Senate would have in any event insisted. These were the definition of a procedure for withdrawal from the League, a statement that acceptance of mandates was optional, and the exclusion from the purview of the League both of domestic issues like immigration and of regional agreements. The first, designed to disentangle the alliance Americans feared, seemed to the French to permit American escape from the obligations of collective security in Europe; the second, designed to forestall an American mandate in Armenia, seemed to confirm American proclivities for isolation; the third revived Japanese sensitivity to racism; and the last, designed to protect the Monroe Doctrine, suggested that the United States, in spite of Wilson's talk, proposed to continue unilaterally to dominate its preferred area of influence.

Tactically Wilson would have been better off had he recognized the national spirit prompting these changes at the beginning of the conference. As it was, forced to reopen the question of the League, he had also to reopen, for the French and Japanese especially, the opportunity to trade concessions on the Covenant for concessions in the settlement of European and Asian problems. The negotiators in Paris, furthermore, treated as they had been to an open display of the division between President and Senate, aware as they were of the Senate's power, not only pressed Wilson hard before agreeing to what they knew he had to have, but also harassed him continually by questioning, sometimes to his face, his ability to deliver what he promised. He secured the changes in the Covenant, but at an inflated price.

In Wilson's absence the conference had approached a point of decision about the most difficult questions confronting it. During the give and take essential in preliminary explorations for common ground, Colonel House had represented him. House's easy way with people, his quick instinct for another's point of view, his sense of *realpolitik,* his manipulator's delight in trading, made him much less resistant than was his chief to the objectives of the other powers. When he returned, the President lamented that House had given everything away. But this was unfair, for the colonel had only recognized those minimum conditions without which there could have been no treaty. Nothing new had been settled. As the conference moved on, neither House's continuing operations nor even the revision of the Covenant constituted the large obstacles in Wilson's way. These were the wills of the deft and resolute heads of the major delegations.

For French security Clemenceau sought spot guarantees. These included the erection on Germany's eastern border of two strong new states, Poland and Czechoslovakia, both to absorb some German land and peoples, both potentially allies of the French against a possible renascent Reich; the creation of a Rhenish buffer state to be splintered off from Germany's west; the cession to France not only of Alsace-Lorraine but also of the Saar Basin, a bountiful source of German coal and iron; and the complete disarmament of Germany. At these extremes Wilson balked. They transgressed the terms of the armistice, the spirit of the Fourteen Points. France could take less, he argued, for the League would arrest aggression. Clemenceau scoffed. The President, he asserted, talked like Jesus Christ but acted like Lloyd George. France had no interest in pious futures. "I am in trouble," Wilson admitted on March 29. "I do not know whether the Peace Conference will continue. M. Clemenceau called me a pro-German and abruptly left the room."

For ten days the conference was stalled. For six of them

Wilson was ill with what was diagnosed as influenza but may also have been a minor stroke. On April 7 he cabled the *George Washington* to steam to Brest to stand by to take him home. To the uninformed in Europe and America this seemed an act of petulance. Those in Paris, whether they agreed or not, were shaken by the prospect of the President's departure, possibly of the collapse of the conference and of a separate treaty between Germany and the United States. House and Lloyd George in particular labored to find a compromise on which Wilson and Clemenceau could agree. What gradually emerged softened considerably France's original proposals, bringing them close to the implications of the Fourteen Points. The boundaries of Poland and Czechoslovakia were drawn generously enough to satisfy the French, but ultimately the conference arranged for the League to conduct a plebiscite to determine the disposition of part of Silesia coveted by both the Germans and the Poles. The Polish corridor to the sea put some Germans under Polish rule, but the President had realized that access to the sea would disrupt ideal ethnographic patterns; and Danzig, the predominantly German city which was to serve as Poland's port, was placed under the supervision of the League. France obtained Alsace-Lorraine, as Wilson had always thought she should, and economic concessions in the Saar, but the League was to administer the latter area for fifteen years and then hold a plebiscite there. For the same period the French were to occupy the Rhineland, which thereafter was to remain demilitarized, but no Rhenish buffer state was formed. Finally, Germany's army was limited to token size, 100,000 men.

In order to persuade Clemenceau to retreat this far, Lloyd George and Wilson had had to propose an ancillary security treaty by which their nations guaranteed to assist France if Germany attacked her. The President should have known, as Clemenceau did, that the Senate would reject so firm an alliance, no matter what its merit. But the wily Frenchman took the bribe not because he expected the United States to ratify the security treaty, but because the treaty of peace stipulated that if France deemed her situation insecure (and failure of ratification would permit her to), she could choose to continue after fifteen years to occupy the Rhineland. This convinced Clemenceau that his country would be safe. Time proved him wrong only because his successors did not elect to exercise the option he had provided.

Though Wilson tempered France's territorial and military ambitions, he bowed almost without a struggle to the combined French and British claims for reparations far in excess of anything Germany could pay. Lloyd George, committed by campaign oratory to astronomical exactions, was also under pressure from the Dominions, especially Australia, to cross their exchequers with German gold. Seeking like balm for France's wounds, Clemeceau worked out with the British a formula that grossly violated the prearmistice agreement to limit reparations to the cost of civilian damages. By defining pensions as a part of these costs, this formula substantially restored the Allies' wartime expectation of an indemnity for the whole cost of war. When Wilson accepted their definition, in spite of the objections of his experts, he still hoped that reparations would be limited by a ceiling of time or money to be set at Paris, but he let the plan persist even after no such conclusion could be reached. He also endorsed the clause, first drafted by one of his experts, John Foster Dulles, attributing the damage to which the Allies had been subjected to "the war imposed upon them by the aggression of Germany and her allies." Given this spirit and the inclusion of pensions, the commission to which the calculation of reparations was assigned had in hand an algebra contrived to produce a sum close to $120 billion, the fantastic British goal. In the decade after the peace, reparations of this dimension became a dominant factor in the continuing economic disorder not of Germany alone but of the entire world, a disruptive subject of continual negotiation and adjustment. With unparalleled intensity they contributed, as did the plausible but painful clause about aggression, to German resentment toward the treaty. It was a measure of Wilson's total achievement that the decision on reparations, the only issue on which he permitted his adversaries their way, was probably the worst solution reached at Paris.

In 1919, however, the President's dealings with Italy and Japan provoked more criticism. With inexplicable unconcern, Wilson had accepted before the conference began the Italians' proposal, a provision in their secret treaty with the British, that their northern frontier extend to the line of the Brenner Pass. This boundary put 200,000 Austrains under Italian rule, an unnecessary violation of self-determination since a more southern line would have been defensible. Wilson did not think to trade, but later he desperately needed bargaining strength, for the Italians, attempting to dominate the entire Adriatic, demanded the port of Fiume, a city completely surrounded by Yugoslavs and vital for their commerce. When the other powers opposed them, the Italians with bald duplicity marched into the city. Wilson's indignant response was appallingly naïve. Late in April he appealed in the name of justice directly to the Italian people. The insulted

Italian delegation immediately left the conference; their people, reacting to the force of moral principle as anyone at Paris except for Wilson would have predicted, roared their disapproval of the President's unsolicited intrusion. Ultimately the delegates returned and signed the treaty which did not give them Fiume, but there had been small chance of this in any case. Wilson's blunder, winning little, solidified support in Italy for an intransigent, deceitful diplomacy and brought the conference, already bathed in truculence, near to disintegration.

This gave the Japanese additional leverage. They had come to Paris to obtain international approval of their assumption of the German leasehold at Kiaochow and of German economic privileges in Shantung, the peninsula across the Yellow Sea from Japanese-held Korea. They sought also endorsement of the validity of their larger economic schemes in China. The Chinese opposed this entire program, but Japan's secret treaties with France and England, the concessions she had wrung from China during the war, and her wartime seizure of German holdings sustained her argument. Furthermore, taking advantage of Wilson's revision of the Covenant, Baron Makino had asked again for an endorsement there of the "principle of the equality of nations and just treatment of their nationals." Makino let the Australians block this in return for British support on Shantung. He also forced his case at just the time the Italians walked out, exploiting thereby Wilson's fear that Japan, too, might depart and thus destroy the conference and the League. The President consented to a compromise which by and large restricted Japan to what Germany had had. In a separate agreement the Japanese promised to return Kiaochow to China. These arrangements upset White and Bliss, but Wilson was doubtless as correct as he was depressed in calling them "as satisfactory as could be got out of the tangle of treaties . . . involved."

This might have been said also of the whole Treaty of Versailles. In spite of secret treaties and armies of occupation, Wilson time and again, in situations of extraordinary difficulty and complexity, had brought his adversaries to incline toward him. Of course they did not surrender, but they granted enough to his vigilance to make the treaty more moderate and just than it could have been without his constant effort. Most of the spirit and the letter of the Fourteen Points he protected. On Germany, as he said, the treaty was "severe," but she had lost the war that she more than any other power had begun, and her penalties, except for reparations, were not unreasonable either by the standards of what she would have imposed had she won, or by those of other great treaties following other great wars, or even by those of the rough, elusive concepts of justice among states. Perhaps peace would have been better served had Austria-Hungary been preserved as an element in the balance of Europe, but it was the war and the developments of decades preceding the war, not the decisions of the conference, that destroyed that empire. As it stood, the Treaty of Versailles defined the nearest possible approximation to an ethnographic map of Europe. This satisfied the strivings for independence of small, dedicated groups of people, strivings from which the principle of self-determination had been distilled. Ethnography interfered with myriad geographic, economic and military necessities in the lives of nations, but even these might have been supplied by the processes of discussion and cooperation Wilson thought the League assured. For as he had predicted, the

League was inextricably a part of the treaty, the instrument — "convenient, indeed indispensable" — for the execution of many of its provisions, the crown, as he saw it, of the conference, "the main object of the peace . . . the hope of the world."

It was, however, precisely the League which, in spite of the amendments to the Covenant, remained the target of the Republicans steeled to seize from the President any credit he could command, the target also of the isolationists of both parties resolved somehow to erase the war just fought, to escape any other by building around the United States an impenetrable diplomatic wall. Unfortunately for Wilson, much that was done or left undone at Paris enriched the opportunities of his opponents at home. The Irish, hamstrung by British policy, still lacked home rule. Most Poles thought their generous new boundaries mean, most Italians saw in Wilson a Judas. And the Germans, their mawkish self-pity already overflowing, took in bad part even lenient terms. Large numbers of each of these peoples in the United States, participating fully in the vexations of their former countrymen, were ready partners in, or easy captives of, Republican designs. So also were those self-conscious "native" Americans, legion in California, who agreed with William Randolph Hearst that the Shantung settlement, selling out China to Japan, bared the West Coast to the Yellow Peril.

To some degree, no matter what Wilson had said or done, these sentiments would have flourished. Their seeds had grown for years. But Wilson seemed almost to cultivate them. Apparently lost in worthy abstractions he could reiterate but not adequately communicate, he had explained neither to the press nor even to his friends and potential friends the reasons for many of his decisions. He retained, in spite of the Italian fiasco, his illusions that men surely agreed with him because surely he was right. And he continued egregiously to underestimate the impenetrable strength of his challengers in the Senate. Less than ever before did the President seem capable of tolerating disagreement about policy or division of authority.

This had hastened the end of his friendship with House. At times perhaps unwisely, but always honestly, the colonel during the conference, abandoning his former restraint, had differed often and sharply with his chief. He talked for the last time in his life with Wilson just before the President left for home. House "urged him to meet the Senate in a conciliatory spirit," to treat them "with the same consideration he had used with his foreign colleagues" at the peace table.

"House," came the abrupt reply, "I have found one can never get anything in this life that is worth while without fighting for it." Certainly Wilson had fought valiantly and successfully at Paris; just as certainly his mood as he departed, like his presumptions before he arrived, threatened as did nothing else the ratification of the treaty, the life of his League, the "hope of the world" he dared not disappoint.

I X

"The Final Grapple of Principle"

1919–1920

Woodrow Wilson brought his treaty home to a people predisposed to accept it. Few Americans were familiar with the whole long document, but most had learned something about the League of Nations, millions were enthusiastic about it, and the great majority saw no serious objection to it. The isolationists, the hostile hyphenate groups, the corporal's guard of antagonistic liberals who thought the President had not done well enough at Paris, constituted all together perhaps a quarter of the electorate. Even more than a receptive nation, a righteous cause, Wilson believed, assured ratification. "In the settlements of the peace," he told the Senate, presenting the treaty to it on July 10, "we have sought . . . only the restoration of right and the assurance of liberty everywhere. . . . The League of Nations was the practical statesman's hope of success." "Our isolation," he added, "was ended twenty years ago. . . . The only question is whether we can refuse the moral leadership that is offered us, whether we shall accept or reject the confidence of the world."

Wilson's own confidence in the popularity and the irresistibility of his League hardened those patterns of his behavior that had already endangered it. This might not have mattered had not incontinent partisanship stood in his way. But as it was, he could neither cleanse the government of politics nor bring himself, as he had in happier days, to adjust his tactics to reality. A telling episode soon after he returned revealed the assumption that especially misled him. A member of the Senate Committee on Foreign Relations, a particularly fervid opponent of the treaty, asked whether the United States could not make a separate peace with Germany, a peace unconnected with the League. "We could, sir," Wilson replied, "but I hope the people . . . will never consent to it."

"There is no way," his interrogator responded, "by which the people can vote on it." The senator was correct. Blink the problem though he would, the President in order to succeed had to enlist two thirds of the Senate, a body he had too long ignored.

This was a difficult, but by no means an impossible, assignment. Of the ninety-six senators, forty-nine were Republicans, but only fourteen of these were irreconcilably against the League. The other thirty-five, resolved though they were to Republicanize Wilson's work, proposed ultimately not to reject the treaty or even to amend it outright, but to approve it subject to a number of reservations. Because the League was so closely identified with Wilson, for partisan purposes the significant reservations pertained to it. Twenty-three Republicans favored the strong reservations drafted by Henry Cabot Lodge, their majority leader. These in varying degree ran counter to what the President believed the Covenant meant. They were designed to "Americanize" that document, to prevent what their sponsors called a departure from national tradition. The remaining twelve Republicans, sympathetic to Wilson's internationalism, preferred milder reservations, moderate statements interpreting the provisions of the Covenant. Since only four of forty-seven Democrats opposed the treaty, a coalition of Democrats and moderates would have commanded a majority vote, enough to determine what kind of reservations should be adopted. Given the state of public opinion, such a coalition by exercising care in what it did could almost certainly have attracted the additional support needed for a two-thirds vote on approval of the treaty with these reservations.

But the coalition could not be formed because Wilson would not permit it. Though simple arithmetic showed the Democratic leaders in the Senate that concessions to the opposition were in order, they awaited the President's instructions. Loyal party men, searching for a winning issue in 1920, hoping that Wilson's treaty might furnish this, they were prepared to resist the Republicanizing of the League unless and until he advised them otherwise. This advice they never received, for the issue, as Wilson viewed it, was both personal and moral. Such an issue he had never negotiated.

The personal complication Lodge supplied. It was Lodge who organized the round robin; Lodge who adopted the strategy of adding reservations to the treaty, a strategy worked out by Elihu Root; Lodge who packed the Foreign Relations Committee with irreconcilables and strong reservationists. As majority leader of the Senate, he exercised extraordinary parliamentary skill to hold his party together and to enhance its strength and prestige for 1920. To do so, he had always to consider the personal strength of the fourteen dogmatic irreconcilables, many of them quite prepared to bolt if they were crossed. But the pressure they exerted did not much discomfort him, for Lodge was resolved at a minimum to embarrass Wilson and the Democrats, and his behavior suggested from the first that he personally preferred if possible to prevent approval of the treaty in any form.

Apart from obdurate partisanship, Lodge genuinely distrusted Wilson's kind of internationalism. He had long maintained that the United States should play a large part in world affairs, but for this he put his faith in a ready navy and army, in manipulating the balance of power, and in unilateral action to hold strategic command of the oceanic approaches to the nation and its overseas possessions. The principle of the security treaty with France he approved; the principles of the League he considered threatening to American sovereignty. He believed, moreover, as did many of his colleagues, that the time had come for the Senate to reassert authority over foreign policy, which, in their opinion, the President had too arbitrarily controlled. Meaner considerations also influenced Lodge. He kept in mind always the prejudices of his many Irish and Italian constituents. He nourished a vindictive jealousy of Wilson. A narrow, bitter, ruthless man whose ways exasperated even his allies, Lodge was nevertheless too adroit and too powerful to scorn. But Wilson recklessly did just this. The President, as despising as he was despised, credited his antagonist with only political and petty motives. If for Lodge the most odious aspect of the League was that it was Wilson's League, for Wilson, the most hateful characteristic of reservations was that they were Lodge's reservations. A mutual, devouring animosity stunted in both men any propensity to search rationally for a compromise.

Aside from their authorship, the Lodge reservations struck Wilson as obstructive, unnecessary and immoral. He objected, to begin with, to the very idea of ratifying the treaty and the Covenant except with unreserved enthusiasm. He held also that the reservations would necessitate renegotiation of the treaty, a contention which the Republicans, the Counselor of the Department of State, and ultimately also the British and the French denied. Two reservations made Congress the sole judge of when and whether the United States should accept a mandate or withdraw from the League; two others claimed for the nation exclusive authority over its tariff, immigration and labor policies, and over the Monroe Doctrine. Wilson argued that the changes in the Covenant he had obtained during the peace conference sufficiently covered these matters. He also opposed a reservation exempting the United States from decisions of the League on which any member and its self-governing dominions cast in the aggregate more than one vote. The American veto in the council, he observed, made superfluous this ungracious protest against the seats of the British Dominions in the Assembly.

Especially he objected to the reservation on Article X stating that the United States assumed no obligation to preserve the territorial integrity or political independence of any other country unless Congress should so provide. This abused what Wilson considered the essential spirit of the League. He had drafted Article X himself. It was, he maintained, permissive, imposing no legal restraint on the constitutional authority of Congress to declare war and to appropriate money. It entailed, rather, a moral obligation, the assumption by the nation of its share of the responsibility for preserving the peace of the world. From this, he believed, there should be no escape; on this, no temporizing.

In the abstract Wilson was probably right, but the things he felt so strongly were difficult to explain even to good friends of the League. Though the Covenant as written indubitably protected American domestic policy and the Monroe Doctrine, Lodge's reemphasis of the Senate's parochialism worked no potential harm. If, moreover, the obligation of Article X was moral, even Lodge's graceless words could not destroy it. His reservation made a great nation seem to deny its greatness, but it left the council free to advise action against aggression and left the United States free to recognize, as Wilson thought it would, the moral compulsion of such advice. What was lost counted less than did the imperative need for compromise. So advised Gilbert Hitchcock, the Democratic minority leader in the Senate, Colonel House, Lansing, Baruch and many others. As the struggle over ratification proceeded, the differences between the President and Lodge seemed increasingly less significant for the world than the prospect that the United States might not join the League of Nations. But Wilson, once again engaged completely in a proposition of his own, thought Satan was his enemy. There was no way for him to let go. There was no way for him to separate his grand vision from his particular phrasing of it, to separate either from his personality and its fulfillment.

This magnified Lodge's tactical advantage. The President did talk individually to a number of Republicans, but his single effort was to convince them to assume his exact position. None did; without openly breaching party discipline, none could. His illustrated lectures drove the moderates, reluctant though they were to go, toward

Lodge. And from each fruitless day the senator drew strength. Holding the treaty in committee for public hearings until the middle of September, he made the hearings a forum for airing grievances. During this period and the next two months while the Senate debated the treaty, spokesmen of every hostile point of view broadcast their case in every medium of publicity they could exploit or Republican wealth could buy. So, for example, Irish nationalists complained again and again, as did the irreconcilables, that Article X invited the use of American troops to help the British suppress the Sinn Fein in Ireland. From repetition alone, this falsehood, with many others like it, gained a growing currency. Lodge's cup of poison filled to overflow.

In another, more subtle and more certain way, time worked for Lodge. Wilson was relying on public enthusiasm to sustain him, but even before he returned from Europe, interest in the treaty had begun to flag. During the war itself, idealism had influenced national attitudes less than the President thought. With the end of hostilities, it cut still less through the roots of selfishness and prejudice. What remained of idealistic fervor for the League, furthermore, was increasingly dispelled as problems close at hand gave world affairs the appearance of remoteness. The dislocation of industrial reconversion made unemployment the first concern of thousands of workers and thousands more of discharged veterans. These men wanted not League nor reservations, but jobs and help, which neither Congress nor the President considered the business of the government. Employed and unemployed alike suffered from the surging inflation that followed the scrapping of most wartime controls. Indeed, Wilson shared the headlines the day he returned with the troublesome cost of living, a condition for which he proposed no basic solution. As prices sped ahead of wages, as management mobilized to restore the open shops unionized during war, as labor tried to solidify its wartime gains, strikes disrupted many industries, including steel, coal, and railroads. In every case, reflecting the popular temper, the administration was cool toward labor. No really crucial strike was won.

Hostility toward labor was only one facet of an insidious panic that gripped Americans. Where they had so recently seen the enemy in everything they disliked — in strikers, Negroes, aliens, eccentrics — they now saw Red. There were some American radicals, some Bolsheviks, of whom an irresponsible few did throw bombs or send them through the mails, but the Great Red Scare was a fabrication of demagogues exploiting the emotionalism war and the Russian revolution had primed. To this, major contributions were made by Wilson's cabinet, especially Attorney General Palmer, who inspirited midnight raids by his own department, mass deportations by immigration officials, gross abridgments of the Bill of Rights — all in all, a revolting, mad, official adventure in establishing guilt by accusation, innuendo, and association. The President did nothing to restrain this. For the solution of postwar domestic problems he, like most of his contemporaries, had largely timeworn and irrelevant homilies to suggest; to the damping of hysteria, he, like most of them, gave little thought. He was preoccupied by the challenge to his League; and in his preoccupation the environment moved past him, not all at once, but at a prodigious rate, reaching in its blackest hours a state that stultified that best spirit of America on which his purpose depended. Unemployment, inflation, strikes and panic, as time went by, diverted from the debate about the treaty the attention a free people owed a crisis in its foreign policy.

Partly to recapture his diminishing audience, Wilson began a speaking trip across the continent in September, 1919. Before leaving, he announced that he would not oppose purely interpretive reservations. Indeed, he prepared a private draft of these for Senator Hitchcock's use. But what he proposed conceded nothing to Republicanizing. On that account he saw no profit in remaining in Washington to direct a strategy of compromise. Resolved instead to overpower his opposition in the Senate, he went to the people to show them the truth as he saw it, thereby to arouse a passion for the League the Republicans could not withstand. There was small chance public opinion would respond as Wilson expected it to. Even if it had, the Republicans in the Senate, most of them safe in their seats for another three or five years, had the security and often the convictions to ignore it. But familiar habits of mind directed the President to his course: in a test with parliament, a prime minister repaired to the hustings. Persuasion was certain there to attend a righteous cause. The ordeal he designed exhilarated Wilson. He had been seriously ill in Paris, tired and overtaxed since his return. But the danger of damaging his health seemed to him a risk he had to take to keep his bond with the boys who had died, so he believed, to make the world safe from war.

Through the heartland of his enemies Wilson's train moved, over eight thousand miles, stopping thirty-seven times for him to address voters in many strongholds of isolationism, taking him through the Middle West to the Pacific Coast, south there, and then east again. As he traveled, larger and larger crowds came to hear him and applaud. Though from Washington his friends reported not

one vote changed, though his attacks on the Senate stiff-
ened his opposition while his absence kept the Democrats
from negotiating with the moderates, the irreconcilables
worried about the acclamation he evoked. And Wilson was
captured in his mission. At times he played on base emotions. "The only popular forces back of serious reservations," he maintained, "proceed from exactly the same
sources that the pro-German propaganda proceeded from."
More often he attempted to explain that the Lodge reservations destroyed the League, that the Covenant as written
safeguarded the interests of the United States. Most gladly
he spoke his heart. He came, he said, "to present a theme
. . . which must engage the enthusiastic support of every
lover of humanity," a theme that went "directly to the conscience of the Nation." "The world," he said, "did not
realize in 1914 that it had come to the final grapple of principle." But it had, "we had saved the liberties of the
world," we could not now "draw back" any more than had
the troops at Château-Thierry. Especially we could not har-
bor reservations on Article X, for it struck at aggression,
at imperialism, at the "taproot of war . . . sunk deep into
the fertile soil of human passion." At Pueblo, Colorado,
on September 25, his peroration epitomized his creed:
"There is one thing that the American people always rise
to . . . and that is the truth of justice and of liberty and of
peace. We have accepted that truth and we are going to be
led by it, and it is going to lead us, and through us the
world, out into pastures of quietness and peace."

Beyond this Wilson had nothing left to say. The ovation of his Pueblo audience surely encouraged him as he
contemplated the speeches still scheduled. In these his message, however rephrased, could only be the same. But these
were never made. Wilson had for days been showing the

strain of his efforts. While his train moved east from Pueblo, he could not sleep. His head hurt mercilessly, more even than it had so often before. Frightened by his condition, his physician insisted he cancel the rest of the trip. The President tried to refuse, but he could not argue with his broken body. Exhausted, despondent, he had to let himself be taken back to the White House. There, too tired to work, too tense to rest, on October 2 he fell to the floor unconscious, the victim of a cerebral thrombosis.

The stroke did not kill Wilson, but it would have been kinder if it had. It paralyzed his left side, made his speech thick, totally disabled him for almost two months, prevented him thereafter from working for much more than an hour at a time. For six months he did not meet with the cabinet; for six weeks he could not meet the minimal obligations of his office. His mind was uninjured, but his emotional balance was permanently upset. As he partially recovered, he was petulant, suspicious, easily moved to anger or to tears. He was even less amenable to reasonable criticism than he had been, less prepared to think of compromise, incompetent to arrange it, unable to assess men or situations or — most tragically — himself. What remained was not Woodrow Wilson but a shell and travesty of him.

Edith Wilson made things worse. Moved only by love for her husband and concern for his health, oblivious to the larger implications of what she did, she kept from him any news that might discourage, any counsel that might upset. Her decisions about what he was not to read, whom not to see, isolated him from the information and advice that alone might have shown even his debilitated judgment its errors. For a time Wilson's secretary, on whom much of the burden of the Presidency fell, in like manner shielded his chief; later he could not pierce Mrs. Wilson's protective wall. No one could.

Wilson was still bed-ridden when Lodge presented his reservations to the Senate on November 6. It was obvious, as it had been for weeks, that the Republicans had the votes to pass them but not the two-thirds majority for approval of the treaty. Senator Hitchcock and most of his fellow Democrats therefore wanted to arrange a face-saving surrender. But Hitchcock had neither the courage nor, in two brief conferences with the President, the opportunity to explain the case for compromise, and Wilson would not hear of it. In a letter to Hitchcock of November 18 the President gave his orders: the Democrats were to vote to reject the treaty with the Lodge reservations, for these were tantamount to nullification. They were then to move the adoption of the treaty on Wilson's terms, either as it stood or with the reservations he had drafted. Though this strategy offered the Republican moderates nothing, both Hitchcock and Wilson hoped they would break ranks rather than let the treaty fail. But the moderates, in turn calling upon the Democrats to concede, had read from the floor on November 19 a letter from the League to Enforce Peace that reluctantly recommended ratification with the Lodge reservations as the only avenue to membership in the League of Nations.

Minutes later all lines held firm. A resolution to consent to the treaty with the Lodge reservations, opposed by both Democrats and irreconcilables, lost 39 to 55. Lodge prevented consideration of the reservations Hitchcock had in hand. A resolution to approve without any reservations, opposed by all but one Republican, lost 38 to 53. The treaty had been rejected.

Yet so strong were the pressures for reviewing this verdict that the treaty was not dead. Most of the moderates and Democrats, stunned by what had occurred, felt they had to try again. During the early weeks of the new year, furthermore, organizations representing at least twenty million Americans petitioned for compromise and ratification. This was the hope of the French and British press, the counsel — delicate to communicate — of the British government, the advice influential Democrats without exception tried to impress upon the President. Lodge had proved he controlled the votes for reservations; it was up to Wilson, if the League was to be saved, to relieve his party of opposing them.

But Wilson, walking now with the help of a cane, existed in a demiworld of querulous fantasies. Intolerant of compromise, he evolved an elaborate tactic, absurd in its original form, alarming even after modification. He drafted an appeal to the people, challenging all senators who opposed him immediately to resign and run for re-election, promising, if a majority of them won, to turn the Presidency over to a Republican. For this scheme there existed neither machinery nor precedent nor possibility. Fortunately the draft was not released. But it was used as a basis for Wilson's letter to the Democrats at the Jackson Day dinner of January 8. It was inconceivable, he wrote, that "at this supreme crisis . . . in the international relations of the whole world . . . the United States should withdraw from the concert of progressive and enlightened nations." The overwhelming majority of the people, he contended, desired ratification of the treaty. The country had to take it without changes that altered its meaning or leave it. If there was any doubt about what the people thought, the clear way out, he recommended, was to submit the question "for determination at the next election," to give the election "the form of a great and solemn referendum."

This pleased only the irreconcilables. The President made the League a party and an election issue, but the miscellaneous conditions, still unchecked, that had weakened the Democratic party before 1918 left it without a chance in 1920. The election could not, of course, hinge on a single issue, and, in any event, a decision on the treaty could not that long be deferred. Habituated as he was to soliciting referenda, hearing as he did the ovation at Pueblo, Wilson had lost touch with his situation. He even nurtured the incredible idea of running again himself with his treaty as his platform. Though he would not seek renomination openly, he repeatedly contrived to make his availability commanding.

Defiantly the President defended his illusions. In spite of his dispiriting letter to the Democrats, bipartisan conferences on reservations made some progress during January, but before the end of the month bipartisanship was wrecked, partly by the irreconcilables, who warned Lodge against compromise; partly by Lodge's own conceit; largely by Wilson, who allowed Hitchcock no latitude on Article X. The collapse of the conferences precipitated a letter to the London *Times* by Viscount Grey, the distinguished liberal statesman to whom Wilson had earlier denied an audience. Grey urged the acceptance of American membership in the League even on limited terms, a position Lloyd George quickly supported in a public interview. But this moved the President only to anger. He added inadvertently to his growing opposition in February by his manner of forcing Lansing to resign. The Secretary of State, as the hearings on the treaty had revealed, was critical of much done at Paris; but he was dismissed not for this, but for arranging meetings of the cabinet while Wilson was disabled. Even Wilson's intimates were shocked by his display of peevishness. After the episode, as his secretary sorrowfully told him, he had very few friends left. He remained, however, the leader of his party, and to its strong disposition to capitulate he administered another corrective. Refusing to talk with senators still at work on compromise, he wrote Hitchcock on March 8, for the guidance of all Democrats, that he saw no difference between "a nullifier" and a "mild nullifier." And so again he repulsed the moderates, again he demanded adamancy.

The President prevailed. The Lodge reservations, revised but in Wilson's view basically unimproved, were passed, on this occasion with some Democratic help. On March 19, the day of the final test, half the Democrats supported ratification with the reservations. But twenty-three Democrats, twenty of them from the South, did the President's bidding. With twelve irreconcilables they voted against ratification, preventing by a margin of seven the two-thirds majority the treaty needed for adoption.

There was no solemn referendum. The President's agents did not choose to expose him to humiliation by bringing to the floor of the national convention his pathetic bid for renomination. They tried but failed to steer through the convention a platform unequivocally endorsing ratification without reservations. The party's candidate, James M. Cox, the favorite of the "wets" and of the city machines, was chosen in large part because he was completely unidentified with Wilson. He supported the League, but sometimes with reservations, and often he concentrated on other issues. The Republican plank on the treaty was all things to all Republicans. So was the Republi-

can candidate, Warren G. Harding, a strong reservationist.
He talked confusedly about organizing an association of
nations other than the League; he enjoyed the full support of the irreconcilables; and he profited from the endorsement of over fifty eminent internationalists, including Taft. Harding based his campaign on his promise to
return to normalcy. Wilson in the first of two statements
on the election asserted that it was a "genuine referendum"
on the League. It was not, but its outcome was cataclysmic.
By a larger plurality than had ever before been accumulated, Harding was elected President.

The new administration never questioned the assertion
that a referendum had been held. After Congress declared
the war with Germany at an end in July, 1921, the Secretary of State arranged to have negotiated treaties of peace
assuring the United States of all the benefits and none of
the responsibilities of the Treaty of Versailles. Without
the United States, the League of Nations never developed
the strength to become what Wilson had dreamed it
might. Outside of it, the United States, captured more
and more by the mood of Lodge and Harding, based its
foreign policy for many years on the precedent of accepting
benefits but not responsibilities. The hope that Wilson
dared not disappoint was crushed, and he was crushed with
it.

Had Wilson died, the Democrats would probably have
agreed to reservations; the United States might then
have been a member of the League; Wilson, a martyr —
his peroration at Pueblo a fitting final testament. As it was,
the imprisoned shadow of a once noble man cast across his
work and reputation a dreadful pall. Possibly the irreconcilables could have defeated the treaty under any conditions, but it was not they who did so. Wilson at his healthy

best brought the treaty to the shoals. Wilson at his crippled worst steered it to disaster. This was sad for him, his country, and the world. But it was evil that irresponsible partisans — Republicans like Lodge, Democrats who followed a blind leader though they could see — permitted it to happen. Wilson's disintegration did not excuse the hollow workings of their vanity.

For a few years after 1920 Wilson lingered, still working when his strength permitted on a platform for his party, a platform dominated by his treaty. But this lingering was empty — Pueblo had heard his last message, Hitchcock had received his last orders, the electorate had rendered its tentative last judgment on him. For in one sense it was on him, as President, that the election turned. He had put the party in an impossible position on the treaty and put the treaty in enfeebled hands. The roots went even deeper than that. He and his associates before 1918 had allowed the Democratic coalition to fall to pieces; he and his fellow liberals of 1912 had little but normalcy to suggest to postwar America; he and they had too long tolerated attitudes that divided group against group within the country, that set some Americans against some foreigners and, with time, turned more Americans against all foreigners.

This was an unintended legacy of Wilson's moralism. His basic, lifelong faith was in the individual as a distinct moral agent, inspired by and accountable to God; in the individual as the special object of a Christian education; in this individual, so accountable and so educated, as the judicious artificer of his own political and economic life. This was the essential belief of the America of Wilson's time, a belief derived from Calvin and Adam Smith and Emerson at least. It presumed, as Wilson did, that norma-

tive man was a kind of William Gladstone, that a norma-
tive nation consisted of a mass of separate human particles, each like him. But within the United States in the
twentieth century, giving these particles a chance to com-
pete was not enough; they needed also help and cohesion.
Particularly in this century, moreover, liberal constitutionalism was not everywhere a possible or an attractive prospect. Some products of Wilson's faith therefore had un-
wholesome, unintended consequences.

The healthy heritage he left has overbalanced this.
Though moralizing confuses, morals do not, nor does
ascetic dedication to the task of governing. The normalcy
of Warren Harding included cronyism and corruption, and
a newer normalcy put influence up for hire. Wilson, in contrast, had no price. Though he trusted the invisible hand
that he presumed gave guidance to men on the make, he
never let these men's revelations become his scriptures. At
the same time, his confidence in the individual as the
proper repository of responsibility and opportunity made
him suspicious alike of special privilege and of concentrated power. The former in many ways he helped to reduce. The latter he resisted rather more than the conditions of industrialism made wise, but with a spirit and in a
prose that helped preserve in the United States a skep-
ticism such as his against the day when public or private
pyramids of power seemed to provide an absolute cathartic
for the modern state. In office and in memory he served not
just the people who elected him but also decency, the dignity of the individual, and therefore democracy.

Nor was this all. In the largest sense the end of his fight
for the treaty did not come with the election of 1920. He
had few friends then; indeed, men had seldom loved him.
But as they ordinarily had respected him, so again they

would. And in his loneliness, in his compulsion, he had always preferred their respect to their love. When he died, men wept for peace; after he died they revered again his principles; they resurrected the substance of those he held dearest — the League in the United Nations, Article X in the intervention in Korea.

Wilson's triumph was as a teacher, his lesson written in the copybooks of generations unborn when he taught. The events of a later time fastened the meaning of what he stood for in the consciousness of his successors in high office. The United States, his countrymen discovered, had to play continuously a leading part in world affairs, had to do so responsibly and morally and in company with other nations. More even than Wilson realized, discussion had to be the substitute for war. For this, while Wilson died, upon his doorstep a little boy, perhaps unknowingly, deposited a rose.

A Note on the Sources

ALTHOUGH THIS BIOGRAPHY contains no documentation, its readers, lay or professional, are entitled to know something about the sources on which it is based. I did most of the research for the book while working on other projects concerned with Wilson's life or times. This work involved considerable reading both in periodicals published during Wilson's years in office and in all or part of the private papers left by him and many of his contemporaries. The periodicals most useful for the purposes of this biography were the *Irish World and American Industrial Liberator,* the New York *Times,* the New York *Tribune,* the *Nation,* the *New Republic,* the *Outlook,* and the *American Review of Reviews.* The most important collections of private papers (all in the Library of Congress unless otherwise indicated) were those of the following men: Ray Stannard Baker, William J. Bryan, Albert S. Burleson, Gilbert M. Hitchcock, Edward M. House (Yale University), Robert Lansing, Walter Hines Page (Harvard University), Theodore Roosevelt, Joseph P. Tumulty (privately owned), and Woodrow Wilson.

A complete bibliography of the published books I consulted would be out of place here, but my obligation to a number of scholars is so large that it merits explicit acknowledgment. This is especially true of Ray Stannard Baker and Arthur S. Link. A friend and admirer of Wilson, Baker brought to his lengthy biography — the fullest study of Wilson that there is — a sympathy for his subject that sometimes overcame his critical judgment, but as an editor and author he put together an indispensable body of documents and data. I drew constantly and heavily upon R. S. Baker and W. E. Dodd, eds., *The Public Papers of Woodrow Wilson*, 6 v. (New York, 1925–1927); Baker, *Woodrow Wilson and World Settlement*, 3 v. (Garden City, 1922); and Baker, *Woodrow Wilson; Life and Letters*, 8 v. (Garden City, 1927–1939). I am indebted, furthermore, to Harper & Brothers for permission to quote from the first of those works and to Doubleday & Company for permission to quote from the third and from Woodrow Wilson, *The New Freedom* (New York, 1913). Indeed, almost all the quotations in this book are from those sources. The others, with one or two exceptions, are from the works of Woodrow Wilson mentioned in the text and from Katharine E. Brand, " 'The Inside Friends': Woodrow Wilson to Robert Bridges," the *Library of Congress Quarterly Journal of Current Acquisitions* X, 129–142, May, 1953.

In equal measure I am obliged to Arthur S. Link. His energy, detachment and insight make his multivolume biography, now well begun, the most authoritative study of Wilson. Particularly in Chapters II through V, but also elsewhere in this book, I benefited both from Professor Link's *Wilson, the Road to the White House* (Princeton, 1947) and *Woodrow Wilson and the Progressive Era* (New York, 1954), and from his direct and expert advice.

Among the other books which I found especially useful were the following: Thomas A. Bailey, *Woodrow Wilson and the Lost Peace* (New York, 1944) and *Woodrow Wilson and the Great Betrayal* (New York, 1945) — excellent studies of the politics involved in the rejection of the Treaty of Versailles; Paul Birdsall, *Versailles Twenty Years After* (New York, 1941) — a brilliant account of the negotiation of the treaty; William Diamond, *The Economic Thought of Woodrow Wilson* (Baltimore, 1943) — particularly good on the mind of the young Wilson; John Maynard Keynes, *The Economic Consequences of the Peace* (New York, 1920) — a dated, acid, but incisive analysis; Henry Cabot Lodge, *The Senate and the League of*

Nations (New York, 1925) — the self-revealing polemic of a self-satisfied senator; James R. Mock and Cedric Larson, *Words That Won the War* (Princeton, 1939) — a detailed account of the construction of hysteria by the C.P.I., and therefore an important supplement to the masterful work of Zechariah Chafee, Jr., *Free Speech in the United States* (Cambridge, 1941); Frederic L. Paxson, *America at War* (Boston, 1939) — a volume rich in data; Charles Seymour, *The Intimate Papers of Colonel House*, 4 v. (Boston, 1926–1928) — the well-edited diary and other writings of the most interesting Wilsonian; and Edith B. Wilson, *My Memoir* (New York, 1938) — the telling recollections of an enterprising woman. I also relied upon materials I examined (but have not mentioned here) and conclusions I reached while writing *Joe Tumulty and the Wilson Era* (Boston, 1951) and *The Republican Roosevelt* (Cambridge, 1954).

Acknowledgments

I owe as much to my friends as to my sources. Four knowledgeable historians read through the entire manuscript and pointed out errors in fact, in judgment and in tone that would otherwise have escaped me. For any errors that remain, I am, of course, alone responsible, but for their generous efforts to save me, I am grateful to Arthur S. Link; to Oscar Handlin, whose advice and encouragement over the years have far exceeded his duties as editor of this series; to Richard W. Leopold, most careful, unsparing and considerate of critics; and to Elting E. Morison, long a wise counselor and perceptive friend.

Above all, in this as in every undertaking, I have been sustained by my wife, who has lived cheerfully with the developing manuscript and the accompanying irritability of its author, improved both text and proof, and provided the while an unfailing example of the power of goodness and love.

JOHN M. BLUM

Cambridge, 1956

Index